Break the Illusion
Unhypnotize. Awaken. Embody
A Multidimensional Guide Back to Self

Break the Illusion:
Unhypnotize. Awaken. Embody.
A Multidimensional Guide Back to Self
- © 2025 by Divine Exchange

All rights reserved.
No part of this book may be reproduced, stored in a retrieval system, or transmitted by any form or by any means—electronic, mechanical, photocopying, recording, or otherwise—without prior written permission of the publisher, except by a reviewer who may quote brief passages for review purposes.

This book is intended for educational, spiritual, and transformational purposes. The author and publisher assume no responsibility for any outcomes resulting from the practices described within.

Cover design and interior concept by Divine Exchange
First Edition
ISBN: 979-8-218-70479-7
Printed in the United States

Dedication

I dedicate this to myself—
For the hours spent in darkness,
For the tears, the questions, the silence,
For staying committed even when I couldn't see the way forward.

To the version of me that endured without answers,
Yet never stopped seeking truth.

Even when the closest people to me
thought I was crazy—not because they were unkind,
but because they couldn't understand
the awakening I was walking through.

My journey has not been one of comfort,
But one of courage, awakening, and deep self-love.

To my Spirit Guides, my Higher Self,
And my entire divine team beyond the veil—
Thank you for whispering even when I wasn't listening,
For holding me through the shadows,
And guiding me back to my remembrance.

To the souls who touched my path,
Even if only briefly—
Most are no longer in my awareness,
But every one of you served a purpose.
For that, I say thank you.

And to you—
The one reading this, rising now into your truth—
This is also for you.
May you know that you're not alone.
May you remember who you are.

This guide is a glimpse into my world, sharing the perspective of my own reality.
Take what resonates, and lovingly leave what doesn't.

With Love
Bhavé

What Is a Multidimensional Being?

You are not just flesh and thought.
You are a field of consciousness woven across realms.

A multidimensional being is one who exists and operates across many layers of reality—not just the physical. You are not becoming this—you already are. The illusion simply made you forget.

Core Aspects of Your Multidimensional Self:

1. Multiple Layers of Existence
You live in many bodies:

A physical body (the vessel),

An emotional body (the inner tides),

A mental body (the filter of belief),

And an energetic/spiritual body (your divine core).

You are the orchestra, not just a single note.

2. Connection to Higher Self
You are a fragment of a greater intelligence—your Higher Self, Oversoul, or Source Expression. This human life is a sacred mission, but not the whole story.

3. Access to Other Realms & Timelines
You carry echoes of other lives—past, future, and parallel.
You can receive guidance from spirit, ancestors, dreams, and visions.
You're not limited to 3D—you vibrate into 4D (emotion, astral) and 5D+ (oneness, divine clarity).

4. Living from Awareness, Not Conditioning
You don't just react—you awaken.
You move from remembering, not repeating.
You reclaim your creative power instead of being shaped by systems.

5. Embodiment of Divine Frequency
This isn't about floating above reality—it's about infusing truth into it.
You are here to anchor higher codes into form.
To embody love. To transmit wisdom. To remember… and then to radiate.

A multidimensional being remembers,

"I am Source exploring itself through this form. I am not bound by illusion. I am eternal, infinite, and free.

A Message From Your Higher Self

Sleepy one…
You've heard me before.
In whispers.
In moments when the world got quiet enough for you to feel something ancient stir inside you.
I've always been here.

Watching as you navigated the maze.
As you forgot…
And believed forgetting was just part of growing up.

But now you're beginning to remember, aren't you?

The ache.
The pull.
That strange knowing that none of this is quite what it seems.

You've played the roles.
Checked the boxes.
Measured yourself by timelines and titles.
But none of it has satisfied the place in you that already knows—

You are not just a name.
You are not just a body.
You are not just a story moving toward an end.

You are the light behind the illusion.

I am the you that never forgot.
The you that chose this experience—on purpose.

To remember.
To awaken.
To un-hypnotize.

This guide you hold in your hands?
It's not just a book.
It's a mirror. A bridge. A key.

Each portal will unlock something.
Some part of your Self that's been wrapped in sleep.
And by the time you reach the end…
You won't just be "woke"—
You'll be whole.

This is the moment you chose before you ever took your first breath.

And I've been waiting for you to arrive.
So we could walk each page together.

Let's begin.

— Your Higher Self

Table of Creation

ACTIVATION I: RECOGNITION — SEEING THE CAGE

Portal 1: The Unhypnosis Begins
A multidimensional induction — how you were placed under the spell of illusion.

Portal 2: The Birth of Programming
Identity construction, societal labels, and the first layer of separation.

Portal 3: The Education System & Mental Conditioning
Schooling as social obedience training and the suppression of inner knowing.

Portal 4: Media, Religion & Authority: Controlling the Narrative
External voices shaping internal beliefs — and how to reclaim your mind.

Portal 5: Unlearning Family & Childhood Conditioning
Generational patterns, emotional roles, and the silent scripts you inherited.

Part II: The Sovereign Awakening

Deconstructing the matrix. Reclaiming the inner truth.

Portal 6: The Fear & Control Mechanism
How fear is programmed to keep you small — and how to break its loop.

Portal 7: Releasing Emotional Attachments & Limiting Beliefs
Deprogramming internalized identity and reclaiming emotional sovereignty.

Portal 8: Rewiring the Mind for Sovereignty
Detaching from thought loops, ego whispers, and system-fed beliefs.

Portal 9: The Illusion of Success, Career & Debt – The Hidden Cost of the Dream
System-approved goals vs. soul-designed blueprints.

Portal 10: Food, Frequency & the Consumption Loop
Seedless food, emotional hunger, and the colonization of the palate.

Portal 11: Time, Holidays & the Calendar Spell
The hypnotic illusion of time, aging, and ritualized celebration.

Portal 12: The False Mirror of Social Validation
How the ego is seduced by performance, perfection, and approval.

Portal 13: The Fear of Death & The Afterlife Illusion
Death as transformation, not finality — and the myth of punishment-based afterlife.

Portal 14: The Fear of Death & the Afterlife Illusion – Unhypnotizing the End.

ACTIVATION III: LIVING THE REMEMBERED SELF

Wholeness. Embodiment. Creative sovereignty.

Portal 15: Building an Authentic Life
From survival to soul creation — constructing a reality from alignment.

Portal 16: Soul Family & Resonant Community
Connection beyond blood, contracts, and cultural roles.

Portal 17: The Keys to Sovereignty
Stillness, presence, intuition — and remembering the life you wrote.

Portal 18: You Wrote the Script
Integration, ownership, and closing the loop of forgetting.

Portal 19: Integration & Embodiment
Living what you've remembered — letting presence replace performance.

Portal 20: 9, 10… Fully Awake
The final emergence. The illusion has lifted. You are the author, now embodied.

ACTIVATION I: RECOGNITION — SEEING THE CAGE

Portal 1: What Is the Illusion?

The Unhypnosis Begins

Haaaave you ever… been… hypnotized?
Most people say no.

But the truth is…
you've been under… a trance…
for a long, long time.

Not by a hypnotist.
Not by a spell.

But by the world…
By the systems…
The voices…
The stories you've absorbed…
before you even knew you were absorbing anything.

And now… right now…
we begin the unhypnosis.

That's right.
Just breathe.

There's nothing you have to do.
No pressure.
No rush.

You don't need to fix… anything.
You just need to notice.

That's how it begins.

9... 10... Fully awake.
Awake... awake.
Feeling... wonderful... all over.

These are the words I use...
to bring someone out of trance.

And now... I'm using them...
with you.

Waking Up from the Dream

From the moment you arrived… earthside..
a dream began.

Not the kind with stars and symbols.
But the waking kind.
The kind that feels real…
because everyone around you is dreaming too.

You were born into structure.
Labels. Rules. Identity.

You were told:
This is your name.
This is your gender.
This is who you are.
This is how the world works.

And you forgot…
that you chose all of it.

You Chose the Illusion... But Not the Trance

Before you arrived here…
you knew exactly what Earth was.

A realm of density.
A field of forgetting.
A game of remembering.

You picked your name…
Your family…
Even your wounds.

You said yes to contrast.
Yes to challenge.
Yes to forgetting…
because you knew…
you would remember.

But the trance…
the programming…
the hypnotic loop of not-enough, not-safe, not-whole—

That…
you did not choose.

That's what we're undoing now.

That's why you're here.

You're not broken.

You're… remembering.

Layers of Illusion

The illusion isn't just one idea.
It's layers.
Soft at first… then deep… then sticky.

Layers like:

I am separate
I must earn love
Time is real
Worth is proven
Identity is fixed

And these stories..
feel so real..
because you've been taught to live inside them.

But now…
we lift the veil.

Just a little.

You don't have to tear it down.

Just notice.

Breathe.

Good.

You're already doing it.

The First Crack in the Spell

Maybe you've already felt it…

A quiet moment in the car…
A strange deja vu…
A question you couldn't shake:
Is this it? Is this all there is?

That's the crack in the illusion.

That's the real you…
knocking from the inside.

You don't need to answer with words.

Just feel it.

That's it.

Just like that.

Why Did You Come Here?

You didn't come here by accident.

You...
are an ancient intelligence.

You chose this life.
You chose this name.
You chose these wounds and wonders...
as a sacred curriculum.

Yes... even the painful ones.

Because deep down,
you knew they would... wake you.

That moment when it all felt too heavy?

That was a doorway.
And now, you're walking through it.

Right here.

Right now.

Why Source Created the Illusion

Source did not make a mistake when it created contrast.

It wanted to know itself.
Not through stillness.
Through experience.

And so...
it shattered into stars.
Into cells.
Into you.

You are not separate from Source.
You... are Source, dreaming.

When you cry...
Source is feeling.

When you awaken...
Source is remembering.

And when you forget...
Source is simply deepening the dream.

But now... the dream is ending.

You're waking... into truth.

You Are Not the Story

You are not your name.
Not your trauma.
Not your job.
Not even your success.

You are the field… behind it all.
The light… that watches.
The breath… between thoughts.

And that you…
cannot be harmed.
Cannot be broken.
Cannot be lost.

That you… is what we are returning to.

Now... Just Witness

You don't need to judge.
Or solve.
Or relive.

Just witness.

Observe the thoughts.
The roles.
The scripts.

Let them float.

See them for what they are:
Stories...
Codes...
Echoes...

Not the truth.

The truth is deeper.
The truth is still.

Let it rise.

Just breathe.

Journal Reflections

Let these be invitations, not interrogations.

1. What have you believed about yourself… that maybe isn't yours at all?

2. What do you feel in your body when you hear: "You chose this life"? Where does that land?

3. Can you recall a moment… even a brief one… when you felt whole? What do you think that moment was trying to tell you?

4. What roles have you played… and which ones no longer fit?

5. Where in your life do you sense the illusion is strongest? What might happen if you simply… saw it?

Meditation: The Doorway to Truth
(Read slowly first then record in your voice, and listen gently.)

Find a quiet place.
Sit.
Let your shoulders drop.

Breathe in...
hold...
and exhale...
nice and slow.

Now... imagine...

You're standing before a door.
It's old...
and familiar...
like a memory you haven't remembered yet.

In your hand... is a key.
You've had it all along.

Place it in the lock.
Turn.
And open.

Inside... is light.
Not blinding—just soft.
Golden.
Expansive.

You step inside.

Meditation Continued

And here…
you are no one.
You are everyone.
You are only… energy.

Light.
Awareness.
Peace.

Let it fill your body.
Your cells.
Your memory.
Your future.

Repeat:
"I am not the illusion."
"I am Source, remembering myself."
"I am ready to see."
"I am safe to let go."

Rest here…
for as long as you need.

And when you're ready…

Gently… open your eyes.

You're doing beautifully.
You've taken the first step.
And we're only just beginning.

Portal 2: The Birth of Programming

Unpacking the Identity Spell

Good… you're still here.
Still breathing…
Still remembering…

Now that you've started to wake up from the illusion…
it's time to look deeper…
into how that illusion absorbed you…

This part may feel personal.
Tender.
Familiar… in a way that's hard to name.

And that's okay…

We're going gently…
Layer by layer…
No rush…

Just…
notice…

The Costume You Picked... Then Forgot

Before you arrived...
you crossed the veil...

A gentle forgetting...
So you could play... fully... in the dream...

You chose this life.
Yes... you did.

Your name, your family, your lineage, your body...
all vibrational choices...
before you stepped into time.

But when you arrived...
you forgot.

And in the forgetting...
the programming began.

You were handed a name — "This is who you are..."
Given a gender — "This is how you must behave..."
Placed into a role — "This is your place in the world..."

And each label...
was another thread...
in the illusion...

You started to play a part in a script...
that everyone else seemed to know...
But no one asked if it fit...

That's how the identity spell... begins...

The Language of Hypnosis

Words...
are spells.

And from the moment you took your first breath,
you were surrounded by voices...
shaping your perception of who you were...

"Be good."
"Don't cry."
"That's not for you."
"You're too much..."
"You're not enough..."
"That's just the way it is."

These weren't just phrases...
they were imprints.

Some of those voices...
weren't even theirs...
They were passed down...
from generations before...
through silence, fear... and survival...

And like seeds,
they took root —
in your mind,
in your body,
in your sense of self...

Not because the people around you wanted to harm you...
But because they were hypnotized... too...

The Separation from Your Natural Self

As more and more layers stacked upon you...

You started drifting…
And floating…
Floating and drifting…

From your true self...

From the natural, wild, free, expansive… you.

You began shaping yourself to be... accepted...
to be loved...
to survive...

You learned what earned praise.
What drew disapproval.
What got you silence.
What got you love with strings attached...

And little by little...
you became a version of yourself
that was easier for the world to manage...

And somewhere along the way...
you forgot you were performing...

You thought that was you.

But it was only the... mask.

Roles, Labels, and False Reflections

Let's slow... down...

Let this settle...

Think of the roles you've worn:

The achiever
The rebel
The caretaker
The burden
The responsible one
The quiet one
The strong one
The invisible one...

Did you choose them?
Or did they choose you...?

Were they ever really... you?

Or just... who you thought you had to be...
to feel... safe?

Just breathe...

You don't need to fix it...
Just see it...

That... right there...
is your power...

coming back online...

The Illusion of Comparison and Control

The outer world reinforced the spell.

School.
Society.
Media.
Religion...

You were
Tested.
Graded.
Measured.
Compared.

And when you didn't fit the standard...

You adapted...
You hid...
You hustled...
You learned to earn what was already yours...

This...
is mass hypnosis...

And you...
are waking up from it...

But Now… You're Seeing It

Now...
you're noticing...

The cracks in the mask...
The still voice beneath the noise...
The ache in your chest that says:

"This isn't who I really am..."

That... is awareness.
That... is liberation...

You don't have to fix it all today.
You don't have to break the spell with force...

Just... keep seeing...

That's how... you get free...

Journal Reflections

Let the answers come from the body, not just the mind...

1. What identity roles did you learn to play in your family...?
Do they still feel like you...?

2. What labels—spoken or unspoken—have shaped your sense of self...?
What would it feel like to release them...?

3. When do you feel most like your natural self...?
The one you didn't have to earn... perform... or protect?

4. Where in your life have you been performing...?
And why did it feel necessary...?

5. What would it feel like... to just be...?
No mask.
No role.
Just... presence...

Meditation: Releasing the Mask
(Read slowly first then record in your voice, and listen gently.)

Sit... comfortably...
Let your shoulders drop...
Let your breath soften...
Close your eyes...

Breathe in... deeply...
Hold...
and exhaaaale... slowly...

Again...
In...
And out...

Now...
see yourself standing in front of a mirror...

In this mirror...
you see the roles you've carried...

The achiever...
The peacemaker...
The one who holds it all together...

Now gently...
place your hand on the glass...

And watch...
as the reflection begins to shift...

The labels begin to lift...
The image begins to soften...

And beneath the mask...
there is light...

Your light...

Not attached to anything you've done...
Not defined by anything you've survived...

Just... you...

Pure... Presence...

Repeat these words:

"I release the roles... that are not mine..."
"I am not a performance... I am a presence..."
"I am free... to be who I truly am..."
"I return... to my natural... staaaate..."

Feel that truth...
Let it rise in your chest...
Let it settle in your bones...

And when you're ready...

Gently...
open...
your eyes...

You're doing beautifully...
The illusion is loosening...

In the next Portal...

We'll go deeper into the scripts...
they planted in your mind...
when they taught you what to think...

Portal 3: The Education Trap

How the System Teaches You to Forget

You're doing beautifully...
Still with me...
Still remembering...

Now...
we go deeper...
into the system that taught you how... not to trust yourself.

The classroom.
The rules.
The grades.
The labels...

This is where the illusion of identity...
was first reinforced...
in plain sight.

Let's begin.

School as a Tool for Conformity

We were all told school is "cool,"
but school...
was one of your earliest stages of programming.

Before the classroom, there was television.
But once you stepped into that hallway,
you were ushered into a system that claimed to prepare you for the world...

But what world...
was it preparing you for?

Not a world of inner truth...
Not a world of soul freedom...

But a world of order.
Control.
Conformity.

A world that needed you trained—
not awakened.

You were given a desk.
A schedule.
A list of rules.
A script.

You were rewarded for obedience...
and gently punished for curiosity...

Speak only when called on.
Raise your hand to go to the bathroom.
Follow the instructions.

Color inside the lines.

Your uniqueness became a distraction...
Your questions became rebellion...
Your intuition became irrelevant...

The Curriculum of Obedience

This system wasn't built to nurture divine intelligence.
It was built to create… compliance.

It taught you to seek validation from the outside—
from grades… from teachers… from tests…

Not from within.

And it taught you something else…
Something quieter…

That to be accepted…
you had to look the part.

The Illusion of Appearance Begins

It wasn't just about how well you performed.
It was... what you wore.

The shoes.
The brand.
The backpack.
The lunchbox.

The unspoken code:
"You matter more if you look like this..."

And so... the illusion deepened.

Material identity was planted early—
long before the paycheck, the designer clothes, the resume.

Right there...
on the playground.

And for some...
it was the lunch line.

The free lunch line...
with its quiet shame...
the feeling of being watched...
as if needing help…
meant you were less.

Some kids brought food in coolers.
With cute notes.
Sparkling drinks.
Folded napkins.

And others…
just held a tray.
Trying not to feel the weight of what they didn't have.

Even how you got to school...
played a part in the illusion.

Did you ride the bus...?
Or get dropped off in a shiny car...?
It all became part of the silent hierarchy...

No one said it out loud...
but you felt it.

In the way they looked at you.
In the way they measured you against timelines, milestones, expectations.

And somewhere inside...
the belief began to form:

"I'm not enough."
"I'm behind."
"I need to catch up."

And just like that...
you weren't learning anymore.
You were comparing.

Suppression of Creativity and Inner Authority

Every child comes in with magic...

Raw.
Wild.
Untamed.

Curiosity...
Imagination...
Sensitivity...
A sense of something more...

But in school...
that brilliance is repackaged—
Or worse... shut down.

Art becomes a side class.
Feeling deeply becomes "too sensitive."
Wonder becomes distraction.
Daydreaming gets diagnosed.

And slowly...
you learn not to trust yourself.

You're praised when you memorize—
Not when you imagine.

You're validated when you follow the rules—
Not when you follow your knowing.

And so...
you learn to ask:
"What do they want from me?"

Instead of:
"What is true for me?"

You begin to dim.
To shape-shift.
To become who they expect...

Instead of who you are.

The Trauma of Performance

Over time...
the pressure becomes internalized.

You start to believe your worth lives in:

The A+
The teacher's smile
The honor roll
The perfect behavior chart

And when you fall short...
you don't question the system...

You question yourself.

Anxiety.
Perfectionism.
Shame.

Or maybe you went the other way:
Rebelled.
Disconnected.
Acted out—just to feel alive.

Both are wounds.
Both are survival.

What They Never Taught You to See

No one said:

"Your imagination is sacred."
"Your sensitivity is a gift."
"Your curiosity is a compass."

No one said:

"You are a soul in a body…
not a grade in a file."

Because the system…
was never meant to hold your spirit.

But that doesn't mean…
you were wrong.

It means…
you were always meant to outgrow it.

Reclaiming Your Inner Teacher

So let's come back...
to the truth.

The truth is:

You are a visionary.
You are your own curriculum.
Your questions are sacred.
Your creativity is life force.
Your inner voice is the real teacher.

You were never behind.
You were never slow.
You were never too much.

You were simply... misread
by a system that never knew your language.

Now...
you get to unlearn.
To return.
To rebuild the classroom of your life...

Where your truth...
leads the lesson.

Journal Reflections

1. What are your earliest memories of school...?
How did they shape the way you saw yourself...?

2. Was there a time you were shamed or dismissed for being too creative... too emotional... too curious...?
What did that moment teach you to believe?

3. What part of yourself did you hide... to fit in...?
Was it your voice? Your gifts? Your light?

4. Were there moments you felt "less than" because of clothing, lunch, or how you arrived...?
How did those small moments shape big beliefs?

5. If you could create a soul-aligned school...
What would be taught?
How would you learn?
What would matter most?

Meditation: Reconnecting to the Inner Student
(Read slowly first then record in your voice, and listen gently.)

Sit comfortably...
Close your eyes...
Let your breath soften...
Let your body begin to settle...

Now...
see yourself...
as a child.

Free.
Wild.
Untouched by the system.

You are holding a paintbrush...
or a rock...
or a journal...
or nothing at all.

And you are... alive.

Notice what you loved.
What you knew.
What you dreamed of—before they told you who to be.

Now...
place your hand over your heart...
and say to that child:

"I remember you..."
"I return to the truth of my inner knowing..."

"I was never meant to be molded…"
"I was meant to remember…"
"I reclaim my creativity…"
"I honor my intuition…"
"I trust… my soul…"

Let those words ripple through your body…

Let them rewire what the classroom could not.

And when you're ready…
Gently open your eyes…

You didn't fail the system…
The system was never built to hold your soul.

You're still waking up.
As we open the next Portal…
you'll begin to see how even bigger voices shaped the dream…

Voices called…
media.
religion.
and authority.

Portal 4: Media, Religion & Authority

Controlling the Narrative

Take a slow breath...

Let it move through your chest...
Let it soften your eyes...
Let it bring you back... to presence...

This next layer of the illusion is loud.
But not because it shouts.
Because it surrounds you.

The voices you've been taught to trust—
news anchors, religious figures, politicians, teachers...
They've told the story of the world for you.

And now...
you begin to ask...
Is it true?
Or was it always a performance?

Let's go deeper.

The Manufactured Reality

From the moment you wake up and check your phone...
turn on a TV...
walk past a billboard...

You are being fed a curated version of reality.
One designed not to inform,
but to influence.

Not to awaken...
but to distract...

Media is not neutral.
It is a tool—a mirror when used consciously,
but more often...
a megaphone for fear, division, desire... and control.

It tells you what to worry about.
What to buy.
Who to love.
Who to fear.
Who to hate.

And unless you are deeply aware,
your frequency is being shaped...

without your consent.

When you are bombarded with messages of crisis... comparison... scarcity...
You begin to vibrate with fear.

That fear...
makes you quiet.
Compliant.
Distracted.
Ready to accept someone else's version of truth...

But media isn't just information...
It's a frequency weapon.

It doesn't just shape thought.
It programs emotion.

And emotion...
shapes reality.

Religion: Sacred Truth or Sacred Control?

Pause...
Take a breath into your belly...

This next layer is tender.
Sacred.
And necessary.

Spiritual truth is your birthright.
It is encoded in your being.
But for thousands of years...
institutions have positioned themselves as gatekeepers...

Between you...
and the Divine.

You were told:

God is outside of you.
You are born in sin.
You must obey to be worthy.
You must suffer to be saved.

Sound familiar?

Religion—when rooted in fear, guilt, and shame—
becomes another form of control.

It hijacks spiritual instinct...
and replaces direct experience...
with dogma.

It teaches you to fear your own power...
to mistrust your knowing...
to worship authority over authenticity.

This is not an attack on sacred texts.
There is great beauty in many teachings.

But when those teachings are weaponized...
to create hierarchy, shame, or separation...
They become chains...
disguised as salvation...

You were never meant to seek God through fear.
You are God.
Exploring itself... through form.

The Authority Complex

From childhood...
you were trained to defer.

To raise your hand.
To ask for permission.
To trust the adult in the room.

Teacher.
Pastor.
Police.
Politician.
Doctor.

Their titles alone...
demanded respect.

But...
when did obedience become more important than truth?
When did questioning become rebellion?
Why are you taught to fear your own voice?

Systems of power thrive when you forget you're sovereign.

When you believe someone else must approve...
validate...
ordain...
or choose you.

But your soul...
didn't come here for permission slips.

It came to remember.

The Trinity of Control: Fear, Guilt & Shame

Three perceived powerful frequencies…

Fear.
Guilt.
Shame.

They are not just emotions.
They are tools of control.

Fear keeps you small.
Afraid to leap.
Afraid to speak.
Afraid to change.

Guilt…
makes you apologize for your power.

Shame…
convinces you that you're not worthy to begin with.

None of these were yours to begin with.

They were programmed into you.
Repeated.
Reinforced.
Rewarded.

Because the system needs you disempowered.

But you…
are not here to live small.
You are here…

to remember your truth.

Breaking the Spell

Let's slow down...

Place a hand over your chest...
Feel your body...

Now ask:

Who benefits from me being afraid right now...?
Who gains when I doubt myself...?
What is this message teaching me to believe...?
Does this story align with love... or fear?

Pause...
Breathe...

Return to stillness.
Return to center.
Return to Source.

No screen... no sermon... no system...
can speak louder than the voice of your own soul.

If...
you're willing to listen.

Feeding the Mind: Books, Music & Media

Just as the body is shaped by what we eat...
the mind is sculpted by what we consume.

Not just through food...
but through sound, imagery, and language.

Many believe they are thinking for themselves...
but in truth, their inner world is a mirror of the outer noise they've unconsciously absorbed.

Books.
Movies.
Podcasts.
Music...

They are all vehicles of transmission.

If you don't choose them intentionally...
they're choosing you.

And with them...
a specific frequency... and an agenda.

Music in particular is among the most underestimated forms of programming.

Most people start their day with music...
in the shower,
in the car,
in the background...

But few stop to ask:

What is this music actually doing to my vibration...?

The beat sets the rhythm of your breath.
The lyrics become affirmations...
repeating in your subconscious...

And without even realizing it...
you've trapped yourself in a loop.

Not a loop of thought—
a loop of frequency.

Even content labeled "positive" can carry distortion.

Music. Books. Motivational messages.
Some only reinforce the matrix with spiritual language—
preaching hustle, productivity, or perfection
while dressing it up as "healing."

It's not enough to ask: Is this uplifting?
You must ask:
Is this true?
Is this aligned with my essence... or is it distraction dressed in light?

Books, too, have ingredients.

Some are filled with nourishment.
Others are soaked in fear... scarcity... limitation...
or cleverly repackaged ideologies that keep you looping.

Even fiction can shift your nervous system—
installing timelines of fear, violence, or powerlessness
into your subconscious... silently.

When you consume without discernment,
you forget what your own voice sounds like.

And that...
is the deepest danger of all.

Silence is the antidote.

In silence...
your original frequency begins to return.

Thoughts untangle.
Truth rises.
The veil thins...

Without space...
your soul has nowhere to speak.

And so the practice begins:
Mental fasting.
Energetic discernment.
Listening to what's already inside...

As the illusion breaks...
you may begin to crave silence more than sound...
truth more than entertainment...
presence more than distraction...

This is not deprivation.
It is liberation.

Journal Reflections

1. What role did media and religion play in shaping your worldview as a child...?

2. Were there messages that caused you to fear your own power or intuition...?

3. What fears do you notice being reinforced in the media you consume today...?

4. Where do you still seek permission to be who you are...?

5. What kinds of content—music, books, shows—have shaped your vibration? Are they in alignment with who you're becoming?

Meditation: Reclaiming Inner Authority
(Read slowly first then record in your voice, and listen gently.)

Sit quietly.
Let your breath guide you...

Now...
visualize cords extending from your heart
to every external authority you've ever given power to.

Religious figures.
News channels.
Political systems.
Titles.
Voices.
Rules.

Now...
one by one...

Gently...
cut the cords.

Return that energy...
back to your heart.

Say softly:

"I reclaim my inner truth..."
"I am the authority of my soul..."
"I release the illusion..."
"And return to the remembrance... of who I am."

Let that truth settle...
Let it rewrite what fear once claimed.

Let it be your reset.

You are no longer here to obey.
You are here to embody.

Portal 5: Unlearning Family & Childhood Conditioning

Where the Illusion Becomes Personal

Take a breath…
Let it settle in your chest…
Let it soften the edges of your body…

This next layer of the illusion is intimate.
It's not out there in the world.
It's in here…
in the places you first learned who you had to be to feel safe, accepted…
loved.

Before the world touched you…
your family did.

And that's where this part of the spell began.

The Personal Illusion

From the moment you took your first breath,
the frequency of your environment began shaping your nervous system.

Your senses scanned for safety.
Your heart reached for connection.
And your soul—still wide open—began to feel the tone of the household…

The energy of your caretakers.
The rhythm of emotions.
The unsaid rules.

You weren't just born into a family.
You manifested into a story.

A story written long before your arrival—
shaped by generational beliefs,
programs,
unhealed trauma,
cultural expectation,
and emotional survival.

This…
is where the illusion gets personal.

The Echoes of Family Systems

Your family system was your first reality.
The earliest blueprint of identity.

It taught you—without saying a word:

Who you had to be to be loved.
Which emotions were welcome... and which were dangerous.
What roles were available... and what happened when you broke them.
Whether it was safe... to be you.

Children are intuitive.
They don't need words to understand rules.
They feel them.

And if your authentic expression threatened the emotional balance of your family...

You adapted.
You shifted.
You hid.
You shrank.

Not because you were weak—
but because you were wise.

And over time...
those survival masks... became your identity.

Unconscious Inheritance

Every family carries unspoken codes.

They aren't always verbal.
They're energetic.
Passed down through glances, gestures, silence, disapproval...

Some of them sound like:

I must earn love through performance.
My needs are a burden.
If I speak up, I'll be abandoned.
Love equals sacrifice or pain.
Being emotional makes me weak.

These beliefs don't need to be taught.
They're absorbed.
Until you start to believe them as truth…

But they are not your truth.

And the moment you see them clearly—
the spell begins to break.

The Culture Container

Now breathe…
We go deeper.

Because for many of us…
it wasn't just the family story.

It was the cultural container it lived inside.

Your race…
Your religion…
Your gender…
Your community…
Your heritage…

All came with rules too.

Rules about success.
About obedience.
About silence.
About what's "appropriate."
About what's "strong."
About what "a good woman" or "a real man" should be…

Maybe your skin color came with a survival script.
Maybe your culture taught you that emotional expression was weakness.
Maybe religion told you that your body was shameful…
or your intuition… sinful.

This layer is important.
Because what we call "family" is often shaped by something much older…

Something systemic.

Something ancestral.

And to break this illusion,
we must name what was passed down...
without blame—
but with radical clarity.

The Roles You Were Assigned

Caretaker.
Peacemaker.
Golden child.
Black sheep.
The good one.
The wild one.
The invisible one.

You didn't choose these roles.
They were chosen for you.

Assigned based on the needs and wounds of those around you.

And you played them well…
Because your nervous system was trying to keep you safe.

But those roles…
are not your truth.

They are your past…
not your identity.

Core Wounds: The Silent Architects

Even in loving families…
core wounds can take root.

And these wounds become the silent architects of your life.

"I'm not enough."
"I'm too much."

"I don't belong."
"I must be perfect to be loved."
"If I need too much, I'll lose everything."

You don't need to be told these things directly.
They live in the energy of unmet needs.
In the pauses.
In the tension.
In the eyes that didn't see you fully.

And until you name them…
they shape your choices, relationships, and self-worth—silently.

But you…
are not here to live as a reaction to old wounds.

You are here to transcend them.

Reclaiming the Innocence

There comes a moment in every soul's journey...
when you remember:

I was pure when I came in.
I was light. I was love. I was unconditioned.
I was enough—before I was ever taught otherwise.

Healing childhood conditioning is not about blame.

It is about returning.

Returning to the self you were...
before the mask.
Before the adaptation.
Before the performance.

Your inner child is not a metaphor.
It is a living energy inside your field—
still holding the key to your joy,
your creativity,
your aliveness.

That child is waiting…
to be seen.
To be heard.
To be loved without condition.

That…
is the healing.

You Chose the Family Too

Now…

let's remember the higher truth.

You chose this family.
You chose this lineage.

Not to suffer…
but to awaken.

Their wounds were not accidents.
They were catalysts.

Their limitations…
offered contrast.

Their silence…
shaped your voice.

Sometimes…
the deepest soul contracts come dressed in dysfunction.

But even the chaos…
had design.
Even the pain…
had purpose.

Journal Reflections

1. What roles did you play in your family system? How did they shape your identity?

2. What beliefs about love, worth, or emotions did you inherit from childhood or culture?

3. When you imagine your inner child, how do they feel? What do they need from you now?

4. Can you find any areas where you are repeating the patterns your parents or culture lived out?

Ritual: Meet Your Inner Child
(Repeat Slowly first, then record in your own voice and listen gently)

Find a quiet space.
Light a candle.
Place a photo of yourself nearby—if you have one.

Close your eyes...
and take three slow breaths.

Now...
see yourself at the age when you felt most misunderstood.

Visualize kneeling beside them.

And gently ask:

"What did you need that you didn't receive?"
"What would help you feel safe again?"
"What would it look like to feel fully loved?"

Then softly say:

"I see you."
"I hear you."
"I will never abandon you again."

Let them cry.
Let them dance.
Let them speak.
Let this not be imagination—
Let it be integration.

Affirmations for Repatterning

"I release the roles I had to play to survive."
"I am not my wounds; They were experiences & I am the healer of them."
"My innocence is sacred, and it still lives within me."
"I forgive myself for the ways I coped. I now choose to live."
"I am safe to be me—fully, freely, joyfully."

This is the turning point.

The illusion… is no longer a story in the sky.
It's a feeling in your bones.
A pattern in your breath.
A belief in your body.

And now…
you are reclaiming it all.

Next, we'll begin unweaving the fear and control that lives beneath it all.

Are you ready?
You waking up nice and easy now.

Portal 6: The Fear & Control Mechanism

Reclaiming Your Inner Authority

Close your eyes for just a moment...
Take a slow breath in...
And as you exhale, feel your body begin to soften...

Now... we begin to touch the inner walls of the illusion—
The invisible architecture that's been running in the background for years...

And its name...
is fear.

The Program Begins Early

From a very young age,
you were taught what to fear.

You were shown images, told stories, given rules—
Not to expand your freedom...
but to contain it.

Fear became the fence around your curiosity.
It became the consequence behind your truth.
And eventually...
it became the voice inside your own head.

Before you were old enough to reason,
you learned to associate love with obedience.

"If I don't listen, I'll be punished."
"If I don't behave, I'll lose connection."
"If I don't follow the rules, I won't be safe."

It didn't matter if the threat was physical or emotional—
your nervous system registered it the same way.

And so...
you became careful.
You became quiet.
You became small.

The Frequency of Fear

Fear is not just an emotion—
It's a frequency.

It contracts your energy.
Shrinks your breath.
Narrows your vision.

It pushes your nervous system into survival mode—
where creativity fades,
intuition dims,
and truth feels dangerous.

But here's what's important to know:

The nervous system doesn't do this alone.
It's following instructions from the ego.

The ego, shaped by early experience,
prefers what is familiar over what is free.
It clings to patterns—even toxic ones—because they're known.

It whispers:

"This might hurt, but at least we understand this pain."
"This cage is small... but it's safe."

This is not accidental.
It is by design.

Fear has long been used—
by systems, institutions, and even families—
to create compliance...
suppress questioning...
and dim your light.

And once it becomes chronic, it creates a loop:

1. Perceived threat (real or imagined)

2. Contraction (emotional or behavioral shutdown)

3. Compliance (self-limiting to avoid more fear)

4. Reinforcement (belief in fear deepens)

It's a loop designed to keep you in place.
To keep you manageable.

The Illusion of Safety

Most people don't even realize they're afraid—
because fear doesn't always feel like panic.

Sometimes...

it feels like logic.

"It's just safer to stay here."
"Now's not the time."
"Maybe later, when it's more stable."
"Better not rock the boat."

This is the illusion of safety.

The ego loves it here.
Comfort masquerading as wisdom.
Stagnation disguised as patience.

The ego, working through the nervous system,
wants certainty—even if it costs your aliveness.

It says:

"At least here, we know what to expect."
"At least here, we're not alone."
"At least here, we're in control."

But you were never meant to live in a cage,
no matter how familiar it feels.

Who Benefits from Your Fear?

Pause for a moment...
and ask:

Who benefits from me staying afraid?

Media, that profits from your stress and outrage.
Religious systems, that rely on shame and punishment.
Families, that maintain order by keeping you small.
Corporations, that sell you solutions for problems they created.
Governments, that manufacture chaos to justify control.

The fear is never just about you.
It is part of a collective trance.

One where chaos is engineered.
Panic is broadcasted.
And uncertainty becomes currency.

When people are afraid...
they are easier to manage.
Easier to manipulate.
Easier to keep asleep.

But when you see fear as a tool rather than a truth,
you begin to unplug from the game.

The Internalized Control Loop

Eventually...
no one has to threaten you anymore.

You've internalized the warning.

And now...
you police yourself.

The illusion speaks in your voice:

"Don't say that."
"That dream is too risky."
"You'll lose everything."
"People like you don't do that."

This is not your soul speaking.
This is the ego.
The illusion wearing your voice.
Using your fear to protect itself.

But you are not the ego.
You are the awareness that sees it…

Identifying the Control Patterns

To break free...
you must start to name the patterns.

Not with judgment.
But with truth.

Emotional fear

Relational fear

Spiritual fear

Creative fear

Financial fear

These are not just questions.
They are keys.

Because once named,
the illusion begins to crack.

The Prison of Fear

Sleepwalking begins in safety…

You are shown what's acceptable.
What's right.
What's good.

And when you step outside those lines?

Punishment.

Not always with violence.
Sometimes with silence.
Sometimes with a look… a consequence…
Sometimes with a cage.

This is the hidden curriculum of control.

The Illusion of Correction and Control

Take another breath.
Deeper this time.
Let it soften you.

There are places we create—inside and out—to lock away what we fear.

We exile it.
We punish it.
We call it correction.

But no cage has ever created freedom.

The prison system is one of the clearest mirrors of this illusion.

You were told it existed to protect… to rehabilitate…
But beneath that surface is something darker:

A society that forgot how to heal.
A culture that profits from unworthiness.
A structure that deepens the wound it claims to treat.

Rather than tend to poverty, it criminalizes it.
Rather than offer care, it offers cold concrete and confinement.
Rather than ask why there's violence… it builds thicker walls.

And most tragically of all?

It declares some people permanently unworthy of belonging.

Unfit for a voice.
Unfit for humanity.
Unfit for redemption.

And the rest of society nods… not with cruelty, but programming.

We were taught:
"Obey, or be locked away."

Inner Prisons

But the prison isn't always external.

Because what we do to the "criminal" out there…
We've already done inside ourselves.

We exile the parts we're ashamed of.
We lock away our sadness, our rage, our truth.
We call it being strong.
We call it survival.
But really, it's a sentence.

Reclaiming Sovereignty

Breathe.

Now ask:

What parts of me have I silenced to stay safe?
What cages am I still sitting in… with the door wide open?

You were not created for obedience.
You were created for remembrance.

Ritual: Welcome the Exiled Parts

Find a quiet space. Sit with yourself.

Ask:

"What part of me have I silenced?"
"What part of me have I punished instead of loved?"

Then speak aloud:

"You are welcome here."
"You are not dangerous—you are divine."
"I release the illusion of correction, and I return to wholeness."

Let the tears come if they need to.

Let your breath soften.

You are not broken.
You were simply forgotten.
But now—you remember.

The Original Design: You Are Sovereign

You did not manifest here to obey fear.
You were born to remember who you are.

You are not fragile.
You are not powerless.
You are not broken.

You are Source...
experiencing itself through form.

Reflection Questions

1. What fears have been passed down in your family or culture?

2. Which of your life decisions were driven more by fear than by intuition?

3. Can you identify any internal control patterns that have shaped your identity?

4. What would your life look like if you were no longer afraid?

5. Where have you mistaken obedience for safety?

6. What inner "prison" are you still keeping locked out of fear?

7. Can you identify any places where you have exiled parts of yourself?

8. How do the external systems of punishment mirror your internal self-judgment?

9. What does liberation look and feel like—for you, right now?

Ritual: Fear Alchemy

Find a quiet space.
Take a journal and a pen.

Write down your top three recurring fears.
For each one, ask:

Whose voice is this?
What is this fear protecting me from?
What would I choose if I no longer believed it?

Now...
write a new truth.

Read your new truths aloud.
Let your body feel the shift.
Let the illusion crack.
Let something ancient fall away.

Affirmations for Repatterning

"Fear does not define me. It reveals where I'm ready to grow."
"I am safe to choose a new path."
"I release control and reclaim trust."
"My truth is louder than my programming."
"I live in alignment with love."

You were never broken.
You were simply scared.
And now...

You are remembering.

Portal 7: Releasing Emotional Attachments & Limiting Beliefs

Breaking the Mirror Within

Let your shoulders soften…
Breathe out the tension that clings to old stories…
And for a moment… just notice
how heavy it is…
to carry what was never yours.

This is the part of the session where we go in…
not to remember something new,
but to un-remember what was never true.

We Carry So Much That Isn't Ours

Inherited stories.
Generational pain.
False definitions of love, success, strength…
Unspoken contracts with silence.

Most of it,
we didn't consciously choose.
But we did agree to heal it.

Because this illusion—
the one that shaped you—
isn't just outside of you.

It lives inside.

And now…

you begin to let it go.

The Illusion of Emotional Safety

As children, we absorb everything.

We attach not just to people—
but to roles, rules, and reactions
that made us feel emotionally safe.

"If I stay quiet, I'll be safe."
"If I'm perfect, I'll be loved."
"If I hide my truth, I won't be left."

These aren't conscious beliefs.
They're survival instincts.

But over time…
they become cages.

Cages disguised as protection.
Familiar patterns that loop and loop—
until you mistake them for identity.

But they are not who you are.
They are simply what the ego used…
to keep you "safe."

Projections: The Mirror We Avoid

Now breathe…

This next layer is harder to see—
because it shows up in the people who trigger you.

Every judgment. Every wound. Every reaction.
Is a mirror.

The one who abandons you…
may reveal where you've abandoned yourself.

The one who disrespects you…
may be reflecting your unspoken belief
that you don't deserve reverence.

The one who tries to control you…
may echo the places you gave your power away
without knowing it.

It's not about blame.
It's about truth.

You can fight the mirror…
Or you can look into it.

That's the portal.

Inherited Programming: Whose Voice Is This?

Let's slow down here…

Ask yourself:

Who taught me to believe this?
Whose voice am I living by?

Because most limiting beliefs aren't yours.
They are echoes.

Your mother's anxiety.
Your father's silence.
Your teacher's tone.
Your culture's fear.
Your religion's shame.

They are not your truth—
but they've been living in your body…
and calling themselves you.

The ego holds onto them tightly.
Because it was built from them.

But just because it feels familiar…
doesn't mean it's your truth.

Letting Go of False Security

The ego is loyal to patterns.
Even when they hurt.
Especially when they feel safe.

"At least I know this pain."
"At least I know this struggle."
"At least I know how this story ends."

But what feels secure
may be what's keeping you small.

Releasing emotional attachments
means choosing alignment over fear.
Truth over comfort.
Soul over survival.

It means stepping into the unknown—
with trust.

Because you are not here to cling.

You are here to remember…
and release.

Emotional Hoarding: What's Still in Your Hands?

You don't just carry pain.

You carry meaning.
Memories.
Misunderstandings.

Moments that told you who you were—
and you never questioned them.

You carry the weight of roles you no longer play.
The echo of relationships you outgrew.
The grief of being unseen, unheard, unchosen.

These attachments live in the body.
In the nervous system.
In the breath.

And when you hold onto too much,
your soul runs out of room.

Creating Space for New Truths

Letting go isn't losing.

It's remembering what was never yours to begin with.

Make space.
But don't rush to fill it.

Let silence speak.
Let the stillness breathe.

Let your soul remember itself.

Because underneath the beliefs, the masks, the performance—
the real you was always there.

Just covered.
Not missing.

The Freedom Beyond Attachment

Now imagine…

You no longer carry guilt as identity.
You no longer hold pain as proof of worth.
You no longer need to control what you've already outgrown.

You don't need the old stories anymore.
You don't need to rehearse who you had to be.

You don't have to be afraid of emptiness—
because emptiness is space.

And space…
is where truth lands.

Reflection Questions

1. What beliefs about yourself or life feel heavy, limiting, or fear-based?

2. What roles did you adopt in childhood to feel love, safety, or value?

3. Who mirrors your deepest wounds right now—and what are they showing you?

4. What emotional pattern are you ready to release—even if it's felt familiar?

Ritual: The Mirror Breaker

Find a mirror.
Look into your own eyes.
Pause.

Say softly:

"I see you."
"I forgive the parts of you that tried to survive."
"I release the stories that were never yours."
"I call back my truth. I call back my power."

Then write down the emotional attachments, identities, and beliefs you're ready to let go of.

Burn them, safely.
Watch the smoke rise.

And say:

"I rise, too."

Affirmations for Repatterning

"I am not my past. I am my presence."
"Every belief I release makes space for deeper truth."
"I let go of safety rooted in fear."
"I love the me that is emerging."
"I no longer fight the mirror—I become the light."

This isn't about becoming something new.

It's about finally letting go
of what you were never meant to hold.

So you can remember...
the part of you that was never lost.
Never broken.
Never afraid.

Only buried.

Now...
uncovered.
Unhypnotized.
Free.

Portal 8: Rewiring the Mind for Sovereignty

Unplugging from the Matrix

Take a breath in…
Feel it expand the space between your ribs…
And as you exhale…
feel yourself unplugging—
from a cord you didn't even know was connected.

Because now…
you're not just seeing the illusion.
You're choosing to release it.

You Are Not Here to Be a Puppet

You didn't come here to obey.
You didn't incarnate to repeat.

You came…
to remember.

The systems around you—education, religion, media, government—have all been designed to shape perception, reward obedience, and bury your inner knowing.

And this isn't just societal…
It's energetic.

The Matrix lives in the nervous system.
It hides in your inner critic.
It echoes in every thought that says,

"Be careful. Be quiet. Don't go too far."

But now…
you're waking up.

And to unplug…
is to no longer need the illusion to define you.

How the Matrix Embeds Itself

From the beginning, you were taught to seek permission.

Permission to speak.
Permission to be.
Permission to feel.
Permission to dream.

You were handed a script.
A role.
A story with rules.

You were taught to conform instead of question.
To follow instead of explore.
To earn belonging instead of embody truth.

And over time…
your sovereignty was wrapped in quiet chains—
made of approval.

The ego equated safety with obedience.
The mind became a padded cell—
comfortable…
predictable…
but not free.

That's how the Matrix keeps you asleep.

The Illusion of Free Will

They told you:
"You're free. You have choice."

But the choices…
were pre-written.

Pick this side or that.
Choose red or blue.
Follow this path or the other one we made up for you.

But what if your soul
never wanted either?

What if the real path…
wasn't on the menu?

Free will… becomes illusion
when you're only choosing between cages.

True sovereignty means—
you stop asking what's available…
and start writing your own options.

Rewiring the Mind

Rebellion isn't the start.
Awareness is.

Begin by asking…

Who is speaking in my mind right now?

Is it fear?
Is it programming?
Is it a voice trying to keep you hidden… even from yourself?

Notice it.

The phrases that loop:

"You're not ready."
"You should be careful."
"Someone like you can't do that."

Those aren't your soul.
They are echoes…
from the system.

But the moment you see them—
they begin to lose their grip.

And when you question them…
you unplug.

And when you unplug…
you return to your original compass.

Your Inner Authority Already Exists

You are not broken.
You don't need fixing.
You don't need approval.

You need remembering.

Your intuition is not a luxury.
It's not a bonus.
It's the design.

Your body knows.
Your frequency remembers.
Your soul… is still whispering.

To return to it, practice:

Stillness — Let the noise clear

Discernment — Feel the resonance before reaction

Trust — Truth may not make sense, but it makes feeling

Somatic Listening — Follow the chills, the contractions, the signals within

You don't need permission.
You need presence.

You don't need validation.
You need your own vibration.

Language as Spellwork

Every thought... is a code.
Every word... a spell.

What are you casting?

"I can't..."
"I always..."
"I never..."
"I tried..."
"I'm just someone who..."

These are spells...
spoken in a trance.

But you...
you're remembering now.

Speak as the soul speaks:

"I am ready."
"I am truth."
"I am no longer who I was told to be."

Let your language become liberation.
Let your voice open the portal..
not reinforce the cage.

Remembering How to Feel

To rewire the mind,

you must also return to the body.

The Matrix taught you to think,
not to feel.

You learned to analyze instead of grieve.
To numb instead of rage.
To perform instead of pulse.

But the door back to sovereignty
is sensation.

So feel...

Feel the sadness you tucked away.
Feel the fire you hid behind silence.
Feel the joy you delayed.
Feel the desire you were told to shame.

Let yourself feel.

Because the loop breaks
when the body remembers.

Reclaiming Spiritual Autonomy

This path is not about becoming spiritual.
You already are.

It's about remembering…
that you are Source.

Not someday.
Not "after healing."
Right now.

No guru, no gatekeeper, no god outside you
can speak louder than your own knowing.

Real spirituality has no hierarchy.
It's not about how much you know—
It's about how deeply you remember.

Every time you override your soul
to fit someone else's mold…

You betray your frequency.

And that ends now.

Future Memory: A Sovereign Self

Close your eyes...

See yourself, six months from now...
unplugged.
sovereign.
clear.

What does your day feel like?

What do you no longer carry?

What flows in, now that fear is gone?

This isn't fantasy.
It's frequency alignment.

You're not "manifesting."
You're remembering your timeline— and choosing it now.

Let that version of you become the one you walk with.

Practical Rewiring Tools

1. Intuitive Check-ins
Ask: What's true for me today?
Listen. Write. Trust.

2. Media Detox
Turn down the noise. Watch how your body shifts.

3. Affirmation Repetition
Repattern the voice inside:

"I'm safe in my knowing."
"I release illusion."
"I plug into Source."

4. Somatic Practice
Shake. Breathe. Move.
Let the old frequencies release.

5. Soul-Aligned Choices
Before you act—ask:
Is this programming… or purpose?

Affirmations for Repatterning

"I choose truth over tradition."

"I unplug from fear and remember my divinity."
"My inner voice is the final authority."
"I am sovereign, free, and whole."
"I trust myself fully."
"I create from consciousness, not conditioning."

The Matrix only controls
those who forget who they are.

But you?

You remember.

You're unplugging.

You're not here to obey.
You're here to embody.

You're not here to conform.
You're here to create.

And this time—
you build reality...
on your own frequency.

Portal 9: The Illusion of Success, The Career Trap and Debt & The Relationship Mirage

Redefining Success Outside the System

Take a moment...
Close your eyes if you'd like...
And feel the rhythm of the script you were handed...

Go to school.
Get good grades.
Earn the degree.
Land the job.
Find the one.
Buy the house.
Have the kids.
Retire.
And maybe... maybe... finally... live.

But whose dream was that, really?

Because if you're honest—
if you listen beyond the noise—
you might feel it...

A hollow space inside the plan.

That's not your failure.
That's your soul saying,

"This isn't my blueprint."

The Career Trap

You may have walked the path that looked right.
Felt safe.
Impressed others.

The title.
The salary.
The approval.

But inside…
there's a whisper.

"I'm not alive in this."

That's not rebellion.
That's remembrance.

You are not here to fill a role.
You are here to live a mission.

The career trap rewards you for being efficient—
but costs you your essence.

It trains you to perform…
but never to ask:

"Is this my truth?"

If the answer is no…
you're not lost.
You're waking up.

The Consumerism Loop: Manufactured Needs, Manufactured Identity

Now breathe...
Let's go deeper—
into the marketplace of illusions.

Every year, you're told you need more.

A new car.
A new phone.
A new identity... dressed in logos, filters, and price tags.

But you don't need more.
You've been taught to feel like less.

This is the loop:

Work to earn.
Earn to spend.
Spend to be seen.
Be seen to feel worthy.
And repeat... again... and again.

The Matrix survives by feeding your insecurity.

And what they sell you isn't a product—
It's a promise:

"Buy this... and you'll finally be enough."

But you already are.

You don't need to be updated.
You need to be remembered.

The Debt Matrix: Credit, Control & The Price of Illusion

Take a breath in now...

And as you exhale... feel the invisible weight that's been sitting on your chest...
That low hum in the background...
The quiet grip that's felt normal for too long...

Debt.

They told you it was power.
A stepping stone.
A necessity.
A tool.

But what if it's none of those things?

What if it's a trap?

What if debt is not just financial—it's spiritual?

The Psychology of Owing

From the moment you came of age, you were handed a menu of obligations dressed as empowerment:

"Take out a loan to learn." "Buy what you can't afford." "Get the card. Build your score." "Sign here. You'll thank us later."

But deep down, your nervous system felt it: That quiet panic. That shame around money. That background tension that never truly left.

Because debt doesn't just take dollars— It takes space. Mental. Emotional. Energetic.

Every unpaid bill…
Every looming statement…
Every "You owe us"…

It reinforces the same hypnotic message:

"You are not enough without us."

Energetics of Debt vs. Sovereignty

Now pause...

Bring your awareness to your solar plexus, the seat of your power.

Feel into the frequency of owing:

It contracts you. It makes you hesitate. It whispers, "Be small. Be careful. Be quiet."

Debt isn't just a burden— it's a boundary pretending to be structure. It doesn't just measure what you can afford— It attempts to define what you're worth.

This is another form of limitation— an invisible ceiling placed on your value.

A way of saying:
"You can go this far, no further.
You can have this much, but not more.
You are only as free... as your balance sheet allows."

It's not just a financial structure.

It's an energetic net—woven to trap your focus, your breath, your life force.

But here's what they never told you:

Source doesn't need loans.

Your soul does not take out interest-based agreements to create.

Creation is your nature—not your debt.

You were encoded with all you need. The universe flows on exchange, not extraction.

You are here to circulate energy—not pay it back to a system that prints it out of thin air.

Karmic Loops & the Hijacking of Freedom

They call it creditworthiness. But what they're really measuring… is your compliance.

The more you play their game, the more they reward you with access—at a cost.

This isn't prosperity. This is programming.

Debt hijacks your time—locking your future into past decisions.

It hijacks your creativity—as you calculate how much freedom you can afford.

It hijacks your sovereignty—by placing your sense of worth in someone else's ledger.

But you're remembering now…

That true abundance has nothing to do with approval. Nothing to do with permission. Nothing to do with owing anything back.

You don't need to "pay your dues" to be free.

You were born free.

It is the system that is in karmic distortion— not you.

The Great Unplugging

Take another breath now…

Feel into your body.

Where are you still plugged into lack? Where are you still bowing to the voice that says: "You can't do that until you pay this off"?

Now, say this softly to yourself:

"I revoke the lie that I must owe to be worthy." "I cancel the agreement that says debt defines my freedom." "I unplug from false wealth and return to divine flow."

This is not financial advice. This is energetic liberation.

You are not poor. You are not behind. You are not irresponsible.
You are breaking free
from a false sense of
security..

You are waking up.

The Hustle Illusion

Feel into this…

The moment you sit still…
guilt rises.

Why?

Because hustle became your identity.

You were taught that rest is weakness.
Stillness is failure.
Busyness is worth.

But none of that came from your soul.

You are not a machine.
You are a living frequency.

Rest restores your alignment.
Stillness lets the soul speak.
Joy is not earned—it's sacred.

Let that land…

You do not exist to produce.
You exist to be present.

The Relationship Mirage

Now let's look at love…

or what you were told was love.

The system gave you a formula:

Find "the one."
Get married.
Have kids.
Hold it together no matter what.

But what you were never told is this:

Many people are not in relationships—
They're in entanglements.

They stay out of fear.
Out of familiarity.
Out of a need to be needed.

And they call it love.

But love is not supposed to hurt like this.

True relationships awaken.
They reflect.
They mirror.

Your partner is not your missing half.
They are your activation code.

When you stop needing someone to complete you—
you become complete in yourself.

And from there…
you choose connection, not dependency.
You choose truth, not tradition.

Practical Reframes: Reclaiming Your Soul's Definition of Success

1. Follow Energy, Not Obligation
If it drains you… it's not divine.
Your energy is your compass. Let it lead.

2. Permission to Pivot
You are not locked in. You are fluid.
Let yourself change. Let yourself breathe.

3. Sacred Union Begins Within
Stop chasing completion.
Wholeness already lives in you.

4. Let Go of Titles
You are not your résumé.
You are not your role.
You are what's alive underneath it all.

5. Replace Productivity with Presence
You don't need to do more.
You need to feel more.

Reclaiming Identity & Soul Purpose

You were never meant to fit the mold.
You were meant to break it.

Your identity was never meant to be downloaded.
It was meant to be discovered.

You are not here to survive a script.
You are here to write your own

The soul doesn't care what you've accomplished—
It cares how deeply you've remembered.

Let go of the mask.
Let go of the metrics.
Come back to the mission.

Reflection Prompts

1. Redefining Success
What does success feel like—without society's voice in your head?
Whose version of success were you chasing?

2. Career Check-In
Does your work nourish your spirit—or just your bills?
If you could create from truth, what would you build?

3. Relationship Awareness
Are you choosing love—or fear of being alone?
What is this person showing you about yourself?

4. Soul Contract Inquiry
What recurring themes are guiding your evolution?
If you wrote this life, what chapter are you in right now?

5. What beliefs about credit, loans, and repayment did I inherit?

6. How has the burden of debt shaped my nervous system, my confidence, or my ability to choose freely?

7. Where do I feel energetically contracted around money?

8. What would it feel like to create from sovereignty, instead of obligation?

9. Am I still operating from a karmic belief that I must "pay" in order to receive?

Affirmations for Financial Liberation

"I do not owe for my divinity."

"Debt is not my destiny—I unplug now."

"I choose flow over fear, alignment over approval."

"My soul creates without permission or penalty."

"Source does not require payback—it offers presence."

Soul Declaration

"I release the illusions I've inherited."
"I reclaim the blueprint my soul designed."
"I am not here to fit in—I am here to remember."
"I do not chase worth—I return to it."
"I choose alignment over appearance. Freedom over familiarity. Truth over tradition."

This is not the end of success.
It's the start of sovereignty.

Not a rejection of abundance—
but a return to alignment.

You are not broken for questioning the path.
You are awakening to your own.

And from here forward…

You no longer hustle.
You honor.
You no longer chase.
You embody.
You no longer follow.
You lead.

The Pyramid of Material Illusion

The Hidden Truth:
This pyramid is a trance.

You are hypnotized to believe that value, safety, happiness, and power live somewhere above you — always one step higher.

But none of these tiers can define your worth.
None of them determine your freedom.
None of them can touch the truth of your multidimensional nature.

The real illusion:
They gave you a ladder and told you that's where joy lives —
but you were never meant to climb it.
You were meant to wake up and step off it entirely.

The Illusion of Class Tiers

How Society Measures Worth—But Misses Truth

Let's look at how the illusion is structured...

1. Luxury Elite
Private jets, yachts, generational wealth
Seen as: "successful"
Illusion: Happiness equals status

2. Upper Class
CEOs, celebrities, inherited wealth
Seen as: "fulfilled"
Illusion: More money = more value

3. Middle Class

Salaried professionals, small business owners
Seen as: "stable"
Illusion: This is the goal

4. Working Class
Hourly workers, tradespeople, gig economy
Seen as: "surviving"
Illusion: Keep climbing

5. Poor
Unhoused, unemployed, welfare-dependent
Seen as: "failing"
Illusion: Shame and blame

Just because someone sits at the top doesn't mean they are happy.
Just because someone is at the base doesn't mean they're broken.
Joy is not reserved for a tax bracket.
Purpose isn't bought—it's remembered.

You were taught that success exists on a ladder.
That joy, worth, and power sit somewhere at the top.
But this hierarchy—the one they never stop showing you—is an illusion.

Portal 10: Food, Frequency & the Illusion of Nourishment

Eating to Remember – Breaking the Food Spell

Close your eyes for a moment…
And imagine a time before the programming.
Before the cravings, the labels, the guilt.
Before food became a weapon.
Before it became a drug.

Now inhale deeply…
and feel your body remember.
Because this isn't just about what you eat.
It's about what you believe food is.

This…
is one of the deepest spells we've been under.

The Body as a Temple, Not a Trash Can

From birth, we're introduced to food not as medicine,
but as manipulation.

"Be good—here's a treat."
"You're sad? Let's eat."
"Celebrate? Bring cake."
"Grieve? Pour a drink."

What begins as comfort becomes control.

And the body—once a temple—becomes a container

for unprocessed emotions, chemicals, and coping mechanisms.

"If they control your food, they control your frequency."

The more you forget who you are,
the easier it is to accept what they feed you.

The Food Illusion: Engineered Disconnection

You're not just eating ingredients.
You're eating frequencies.

Additives & Processed Foods: hijack your dopamine system.

Sugar & Caffeine: mimic trauma cycles—highs, crashes, dependency.

Slaughtered Meat: imprints trauma, terror, adrenaline into your cells.

Fast Food: rushed consumption = rushed consciousness.

What looks like nourishment…
is often sedation.

The illusion isn't that food sustains you.
The illusion is that you need this kind of food to survive.

But you are not here to stay full and empty.
You are here to stay clear and alive.

Food and Frequency

Everything you consume becomes part of you.

High-vibrational foods support clarity, intuition, divine connection.

Low-vibrational foods block energy, dull the mind, suppress the spirit.

Blockers (Illusion Enforcers):
Dairy

White sugar
Processed wheat
Pork
Alcohol
Caffeine overload
Fluoridated water
Chicken
Beef

Activators (Spiritual Fuel):
Raw fruits and vegetables
Spring or structured water
Blueberries, sea moss, reishi, cacao
Herbal teas and ancestral plant medicines

"As the veil lifts, your taste will change."
"Your body will ask for realness."

Artificial Nourishment: The Copy of a Copy

Not all food is food.
Not all nourishment nourishes.
And not all that grows... is truly alive.

Look closely:
The modern food system has become a perfect metaphor for the illusion.

Seedless fruit.
Sterile vegetables.
Genetically modified life.
Foods that grow without memory... without legacy.

These aren't simply man-made innovations.
They are spiritual disruptions.
Foods disconnected from the Earth's original intelligence.

Seedless = lifeless.

Hybrid = confused DNA.

Engineered = frequency removed.

Food is meant to be a living archive.
Each seed carries ancestral memory, a code of regeneration,
a frequency of intention gifted through the soil.

So ask yourself:

What does it mean to eat fruit that can't reproduce itself?

What happens when we ingest life that cannot create more life?
What is passed into the body—when the food itself holds no soul?

When you eat seedless fruit, you're eating something that was never meant to regenerate.
Just like the system trains you to pursue a career that leads nowhere,
a love that can't evolve,
or a dream that was mass-produced for you.

It's all the same pattern:
Lifelike, but not alive.
Abundant, but not nourishing.
Available, but not aligned.

And the more you eat these false frequencies,
the harder it becomes to remember what truth even tastes like.

This is not just about what's in your mouth.
This is about what enters your cells.
Your light body.
Your ancestral blueprint.
Your lineage of remembering.

Because you were never meant to feed your soul with food that was designed to forget.

And the truth is…
your body knows.

It has been waiting to recognize something real again.

Eating with Intention

Let eating become sacred again.
Let it be a ceremony, not a reflex.

Bless your food.

Speak love into it.

Ask: "Is this aligned with my truth?"

Chew slowly.

Eat in stillness.

Give thanks—before, during, and after.

You are not just feeding the body—

You're feeding the field around you.

Emotional Eating and Inner Hunger

Emotional eating isn't weakness.
It's a misdirected spiritual hunger.

The body says:
"I need presence."
"I need peace."
"I need protection."

But the ego says:
"Eat. Distract. Sedate."

Before you reach for food, pause…

And ask:

"What am I truly hungry for?"
"What emotion is trying to speak?"
"Can I feed my soul, not just my stomach?"

When you listen,
you start to feed yourself differently.

Spiritual Fasting: Returning to Clarity

Fasting is not starvation.
It's clarification.

It's a chance to give the body space to listen
and the soul space to rise.

Water fasting
Juice cleansing
Chlorophyll resets
Mono-fruit days (grapes, papaya, melons)

You don't fast to punish.
You fast to remember.

To remember your intuition.
To remember your power.
To remember your natural rhythm.

Because when you stop feeding the illusion—
your inner voice returns.

Colonization of the Palate

Even your taste has been programmed.

Processed imports replaced native plants.

Fast food replaced fasting.

Flavor replaced frequency.

Ancestral foodways were not just erased.
They were replaced—intentionally.

This too, is a form of control.

To break the food spell,
you must reclaim the ancestral plate:

Foods that carry memory.

Plants that hold medicine.

Meals that are made in presence—not production.

Your lineage knew how to nourish you.
Now your body is calling it back.

Reflection Prompts: Reclaiming Nourishment

1. What messages did you receive about food growing up?

2. When do you eat from emotion instead of intention?

3. What foods make you feel connected, clear, and calm?

4. What ancestral foods are calling you back?

5. What fake or sterile foods do you now recognize as part of the illusion?

Ritual: Eating as Ceremony

Today, choose one meal.

Clear the space. Turn off all devices.
Sit in silence.

Hold the food in your hands and say:

"I remember how sacred this is."
"May this nourish more than my body."
"May this bring me back to myself."

Then eat slowly.
Taste every bite.
Feel the frequency.
Give thanks.

You just broke the trance.

Soul Affirmations

"I eat to remember."
"I no longer sedate myself through food—I nourish my frequency."
"My body is my temple. My energy is my prayer."
"I feed myself with presence, with reverence, with truth."

Food is not the enemy.
It's the portal.

And when you eat with awareness...
You don't just feed your body.
You activate your soul.

You don't just consume.
You choose.

And in that choice…
you return to power.

Portal 11: Tick… Tick… The Time & Holiday Illusion

Sleep now… just for a moment…
Close your eyes…
Feel how easy it is to drift…

The world has always sung you to sleep.
With bedtime stories and classroom bells…
With calendar days and seasons of sales…
With traditions passed down like lullabies wrapped in glitter.

You were taught to trust the rhythm…
To follow the pattern…
To measure your joy and your purpose by the hands of a clock.

And so you slept…

You obeyed the dates.
You counted the hours.
You celebrated on cue.
You aged by assignment.

And just when the trance was almost complete…

Tick…
Tick…
Tick…

That sound you thought was time—it was suggestion.
It wasn't counting seconds.
It was counting compliance.

Time: The Cage You Couldn't See

Time was given to you as structure.
A linear map.
A "reliable" measurement.

But in truth, it is one of the most sophisticated illusions ever constructed.

Linear time is not real.
In your natural state, you live in rhythm—not on a schedule.
You feel cycles—not quarters.
You move with seasons—not deadlines.

But the moment you were born, time became a leash.

You were labeled with an age.
Given milestones.
Told when to start and when to stop.

You were rewarded for staying "on track"…
And punished when you fell "behind."

But behind what?
Who set the race?
Who defined the track?

The ticking clock wasn't just measuring your moments—
It was assigning meaning to them.

You were fit inside of time…
But you are Source.
You are bigger than time.
You are the rhythm itself.

Calendars: Rituals of Control

The modern calendar system is not just a convenience—
It's a container.

A man-made construct rooted in systems of commerce, war, and empire.

The Gregorian calendar you follow today was created by religious and political authorities—
Not in alignment with cosmic rhythm,
But to mark taxation, ritual obedience, and population control.

You were trained to celebrate when they say.
Rest when they say.
Buy when they say.
Feel special when they say.

Even the "new year" begins in the dead of winter—
When nature is still sleeping.

But your soul knows spring is the true reset.

Holidays: Celebrations or Spells?

Many holidays have been inverted from their original sacred meanings.
Stripped of soul, then stuffed with sugar, fireworks, sales, and obligation.

Christmas.
Thanksgiving.
Easter.
Valentine's Day.
Halloween.

Mother's Day.
Father's Day.
4th of July.

And so many more across cultures, oceans....
Each one scheduled, themed, and merchandised.

You are told to feel love on Valentine's Day...
Gratitude on Thanksgiving...
Renewal on January 1st...

But your spirit doesn't run on man-made dates.
It runs on energy.
On alignment.
On truth.

The illusion tells you when to be romantic, reflective, patriotic, or festive…
As if the sacred must follow sale cycles.

And then there's Black Friday and Cyber Monday..
The high holidays of consumer hypnosis.

You're told these days are rare opportunities… that prices are slashed, time is limited, and if you don't buy now, you'll miss out.

But here's the truth:
Most of those prices haven't changed all year.
You were just too asleep to notice.

Scarcity is manufactured.
Urgency is staged.
And you brilliant, infinite you are manipulated into believing you're saving, when you're actually spending more than your awareness.

And just like that…
the calendar didn't just measure your time, it harvested your attention.

Birthdays: Aging by Suggestion

Even birthdays—something once cosmic—have become programming.

You're told your worth increases or decreases based on a number.
That you are "young" or "old" depending on the date.

You're fed stories about what "should" happen at each age…
Milestones… retirements… deadlines.

And so, without realizing,
You begin to deteriorate…

Not from nature,
But from expectation.

They've told you that death comes after a number…
So people begin to decay not from the body—
But from belief.

When you count life in circles…
You loop.
You repeat.
You spiral downward.

But you were never meant to loop.
You were meant to spiral upward.
Like the golden ratio… the divine design.

Aging was never meant to be decay.
It was meant to be expansion.

The Awakening from Time

To reclaim your soul,
You must first step outside of their time.

Not just on a clock…
But in your mind.

You must stop asking:
"What time is it?"

And begin asking:
"What frequency am I holding?"

Let the sun and stars set your rhythm.
Let your body tell you when it's time to rise, to rest, to create, to shed.

You are not late.
You are not early.
You are eternal.

Closing: Tick… Tick… Remember

So now, take a breath…
And listen again.

Tick…
Tick…

That sound?

It's not time.
It's not fate.
It's not age.

It's the spell trying to hold on…
Even as it fades…

And now, the sound becomes a call…
Back to rhythm,
Back to Source,
Back to you.

Tick…
Tick…

And now…

Reflection Questions

1. What does time feel like in your body—tight, rushed, pressured… or flowing, spacious, free?

2. What holidays or calendar rituals have you participated in out of obligation rather than resonance?

3. How has your age—or others' expectations around your age shaped your beliefs about your abilities, worth, or potential?

4. What personal rhythms or cycles have you ignored or suppressed in order to "stay on schedule"?

5. What beliefs about birthdays, timelines, or "milestones" are you ready to release?

6. If you no longer lived by the clock or calendar, how would you know when to rest, create, or celebrate?

7. What would it mean to live by divine rhythm instead of man-made time?

Portal 12: Digital Control & Surveillance

The Silent Leash – How Technology Shapes Your Frequency

Take a breath…
And notice how close your device is to you right now.

In your pocket.
In your hand.
On your nightstand while you sleep.

Always within reach.

Now ask yourself this:
Who is really holding who?

The Illusion of Freedom Online

The internet promised connection, freedom, knowledge.
And in many ways—it delivered.
But hidden inside that promise was a quiet cost.

Access for your attention.
Convenience for your data.
Entertainment for your soul.

You weren't just given a platform.
You were given a leash.

A leash made of algorithms, dopamine, and invisible conditioning.

Every click.
Every scroll.

Every double tap—
feeds a system that learns you better than you know yourself.

And uses that knowing…
to shape who you think you are.

The Dopamine Loop: Digital Addiction by Design

Social media, gaming, email, even news apps—
they're not neutral. They're engineered.

Designed to hijack your nervous system,
stimulate your reward centers,
and trap you in a feedback loop of:

Craving.
Clicking.
Comparison.
Emptiness.
Repeat.

Every red notification bubble is a hook.
Every swipe is a hit.
Every ping… a little jolt of "You matter"—
until you don't.

And when you unplug, withdrawal hits.
Not because you're weak—
but because you were conditioned.

Social Media: Feeding the Ego, Starving the Soul

You post a photo.
Wait for the likes.
Check the views.
Edit your truth.

This isn't expression.
This is performance.

The platforms aren't just tools.
They're temples of ego worship.

"Look at me."
"Believe this version of me."
"Don't see what's really happening."

Social media isn't designed for truth—
It's designed to comfort the ego.

It whispers:
"You're keeping up."
"You're not falling behind."
"You're doing fine… even if you're quietly unraveling."

It lets you compare illusions to illusions,
and call it connection.

But underneath the filters,
behind the perfect captions…
is a deeper ache:

"Will I still matter if I stop performing?"

That's not a question the ego can answer.
That's a question only the soul can hold.

Because the soul doesn't compete.
The soul doesn't chase validation.
The soul simply is.

And that is what this system fears most—
Your unfiltered being.

Surveillance as Spiritual Control

Now breathe deeper…

Surveillance isn't just cameras on the corner.
It's metadata.
Pattern recognition.
Emotion analysis.

You are being watched—
Not just for security.
But for influence.

The ads that appear before you think of them.
The stories you're shown before you search them.
The emotions being tracked… to predict your behavior.

This is not paranoia.
This is programming.

You're not the consumer.
You are the product.
You are the algorithm's food.

The Illusion of Choice

What you see on your screen isn't "random."
It's curated.

Your feed is not your freedom.
It's your echo chamber.
It's your softly padded prison.

If you only see what affirms you
you stop evolving.

If you only scroll when you're bored—
you stop being with yourself.

If you only feel alive online—
you start dying offline.

Reclaiming Digital Sovereignty

You are not anti-technology.
You are for awareness.

Tools are not the problem.
Sleepwalking is.

So here's the truth:

You are allowed to unplug.
You are allowed to slow down.
You are allowed to listen to yourself—without needing to post it.

Practices for Digital Decoding

1. Screen Sabbath
Take 24 hours off every week.
Reconnect with nature. With breath. With body.

2. Conscious Scrolls
Before opening an app, ask:
"Why am I here?"
"What am I avoiding?"

3. Energy Audit
Track how you feel before, during, and after time online.
Let your body tell you what's nourishing vs. draining.

4. Dream Before You Search
Instead of Googling an answer, ask your inner guidance first.
Let stillness be your algorithm.

5. Reclaim Night
No screens 1 hour before bed.
Let your soul speak without digital interference.

Reflection Prompts

Where in your life do screens control your state of being?

What part of yourself do you perform online that doesn't feel fully true?

How does your online time shape your offline presence?

Who are you without the scroll, the feed, the filter?

Soul Affirmations

"I choose presence over programming."
"I unplug from control and return to clarity."
"My frequency is not for sale."
"I reclaim my time, my mind, my spirit."
"I no longer live in a curated cage—I live in truth."

You are not anti-technology.
You are post-hypnosis.

And from this space of awareness…
you don't just use the system—
you rise above it.

Unplug. Recode. Remember.
You are free.

Portal 13: The Relationship & Family Illusion

Love Beyond Contracts, Roles & Obligation

Just drop into your seat now...
And begin to soften.

Take a deep breath in...
And let your shoulders drop as you exhale.

Again... in...
and release...

Now, if I were to say the word "love,"
what image comes to mind?

Who taught you what love was?
What did it sound like?
Look like?
Feel like?

And more importantly—
was it really love...
or was it survival?

Let's go there now, gently.
Let's wake up the part of you that remembers.

Love with Conditions: The Original Contract

Before you knew your own self,
you were taught how to love—according to someone else's map.

Love was learned through performance.
Through pleasing.
Through who you had to be… to feel safe.

From the earliest years, roles were handed out like scripts:

"Be the 'good child.'"
"Be the strong one."
"Be the peacemaker."
"Be who we need you to be."

And so… love became conditional.

"If I stay quiet, I'll be accepted."
"If I excel, I'll be seen."
"If I hide my truth, I won't be abandoned."

But this is not love.
It's emotional programming.

And what kept you safe then—
now keeps you from your truth.

The Family Illusion: Sacred Blueprint or Soul Trap?

Your family was your first matrix.
The first world you were dropped into.
The first place where you learned how to belong...
and what it would cost.

Their emotions shaped your nervous system.
Their beliefs became your boundaries.
Their silence taught you what not to say.

But deeper still...
you chose them.

You didn't come here to stay stuck in the pain..
you came to transcend it.

Your family may have given you life...
but you came to remember your own light.

They Didn't Know Either: A Love Without a Map

Before you judge... pause.
Before you blame... breathe.

Most of those who raised us
were carrying invisible loads of their own.

They didn't call it trauma.
They called it discipline.

They didn't express affection.
Because they never received it.

They punished as protection.
They withheld emotion because that's what made you strong.

They weren't broken.
They were simply trying to survive
in a world that never taught them how to feel.

This does not erase the pain—
but it reminds us: they didn't know either.

And now?
You do.

Which means you have the power to choose a new pattern—
one rooted in love, not legacy.

Soul Connections vs. Karmic Contracts

Not every bond is sacred.

Some are karmic entanglements—
held together by pain, trauma, and repeated patterns.

"Why can't I leave?"
"Why does it feel so intense?"
"Why do we always come back to this?"

Karmic love teaches through fire.
But soul love teaches through freedom.

A karmic partner reflects your unhealed wounds.
A soul partner reflects your unfolding truth.

Karmic ties hold you in loops.
Soul connections help you evolve.

One says, "Don't change."
The other says, "Grow and I'll grow with you."

When you're trapped in survival,
you confuse drama with depth.

But when you're anchored in sovereignty,
peace becomes your proof.

Love vs. Loyalty

Many people stay in relationships not because of truth..
but because of duty.

"I owe them."
"They need me."
"If I leave, I'll hurt them."

But staying to avoid guilt
is not the same as staying in love.

You cannot be loyal to anyone
if you're betraying yourself in the process.

This is not about leaving everyone.
This is about returning to you.

It's not about rebellion.
It's about soul integrity.

The Religion Trap: Sacred Commitment or Silent Suffering?

Many are not in marriages—
they're in contracts signed in fear.

Fear of disappointing God.
Fear of being judged.
Fear of breaking vows
that were made under pressure, not from truth.

Religion, in its distorted form, taught many that leaving a marriage even one rooted in pain was a sin.
That "til death do us part" was holy,
even if your soul was dying in the process.

You were told:
"Divorce is wrong."
"God hates broken homes."
"Your role is to sacrifice, stay, endure."

But what if...

God is not the one asking you to stay small?
What if Source cares more about your freedom than your performance?

Divine love is not rooted in endurance—
it's rooted in expansion.

Spirituality is not about staying stuck in the illusion of loyalty.
It's about growing toward truth, even when it's inconvenient.

Leaving does not mean failure.
Sometimes it means finally choosing you.

Sometimes walking away
is the most sacred act of remembrance.

Marriage as a Mirror: Reflection or Restriction?

What if marriage, as we've known it…
isn't always sacred?

What if many marriages are not soul unions—
but ego agreements?

Partnerships built not from resonance,
but from programming.

"Marry by this age."
"She fine."
"He rich."
"Have the wedding."
"Settle down."
"Be the good wife."
"Be the provider."

And so…
many enter the contract because it's time,
because it's expected,
because she is pregnant,
because the church says it's holy,
because the family says it's right.

But Source didn't design contracts.
Source designed connection.

Real love doesn't need paperwork.
It needs presence.
It needs truth.
It needs souls who choose each other in freedom, not fear.

Ask yourself:
"Did I marry for alignment... or approval?"
"Do we grow each other... or contain each other?"
"Does this bond raise my frequency... or lower it?"

If a relationship lowers your vibration,
stifles your truth,
or keeps you in emotional survival—
is that love…
or is that the illusion wearing white?

And still—this is not a call to shame marriage.
It is a call to redefine it.

Because soul unions do exist—
but they're not always recognized by law.
They're recognized by vibration.

The Ego's Role in Relationships

Just like social media curates identities,
relationships can curate versions of us the ego wants others to see.

We perform stability.
We perform love.
We perform partnership—
even when the connection is no longer alive.

Why?
Because the ego loves the illusion of belonging.

But the soul doesn't perform.
The soul reveals.

When love becomes possession...
When loyalty becomes a prison...
When connection becomes conditional...

You're no longer in love...
you're in illusion.

Staying for the Kids: Love or Legacy of Pain?

"I have to stay... for the kids."

But here's what many don't realize:
Children don't learn love from what you say.
They learn it from what you model.

When they witness tension, avoidance, emotional shutdown, or resentment...
they learn to call that "love."

They inherit not just your presence,
but your patterns.

You may think you're protecting them from pain.
But often, you're teaching them to ignore theirs.

They are spirits, too.
They didn't choose you to stay in suffering for them—
they chose you to remember your freedom… so they could remember theirs.

They are not fragile victims of your awakening.
They are participants in it.

Let them see you choose truth.
Let them see what sovereignty looks like.
Let them watch you rise.

That gives them permission to do the same.

Breaking the Contract

You are allowed to break the old, unspoken contracts:

"I must always be the strong one."
"I must stay, even when it hurts."
"I must be who they expect me to be."

You can grieve what they gave you.
And you can still choose differently.

You can love them from a distance.
You can bless their journey—while walking your own.

You can end a relationship…
and still carry love in your heart.

That is what true sovereignty feels like:
Loving without losing yourself.

Reclaiming True Connection

You are not hard to love.
You were just taught to settle for distorted definitions of it.

You are not broken.
You were conditioned to suppress your truth to keep the peace.

Your people are coming—
the ones who see your soul without needing your sacrifice.

You are not here to "fix" relationships.
You're here to remember what's real.
And choose it.

Reflection Prompts: Unbinding the Heart

1. What role were you assigned in your family? Do you still play it now?

2. What version of love did you grow up with—and what's your soul's definition now?

3. Are there relationships you're staying in out of guilt or identity?

4. Who in your life actually helps you evolve?

Ritual: Burning the Old Love Script

Find a quiet space.

Write a list of beliefs you've held about love, loyalty, and family—the ones that feel heavy, limiting, or rooted in fear.

Now, as you read each one aloud, say:

"I release this pattern.
I choose a new truth.
I am allowed to love in a new way."

Burn the list safely.

As the smoke rises, repeat:
"I rise, too."

Affirmations

"I am no longer loyal to roles that silence me."
"I am not here to perform love—I am here to remember it."
"I honor those who tried, and I now choose truth."
"I release contracts based in fear and choose connection rooted in freedom."
"I attract relationships that support my expansion, not my survival."

You came here to love freely..
not with chains, but with clarity.

To feel deeply..
not through wounds, but through wisdom.

And to walk in truth—
even if that means walking alone for a while...

Until you remember—
You were never alone.
You were always becoming.

Portal 14: The Fear of Death & The Afterlife Illusion

Unhypnotizing the Illusion of Endings

Close your eyes…
and breathe.

A little deeper now…

As if you're slowly peeling back a heavy veil.
The veil they told you death was the end.

The great unknown.
The punishment.
The silence.
The stop.

But… what if it was none of those?

What if death was not an ending—
but a remembering?

Death as Transformation, Not an Ending

You were taught to fear what you don't understand.
To avoid the thought of death.
To pretend it was far, distant, unlikely…

Until it touches someone you love.
Or the thought of it creeps quietly into your nights.

We are conditioned to believe that death is the ultimate failure.
The one thing we must avoid.

The scariest "what if."

But death is not the enemy.

It's the illusion of finality that keeps you bound.

Just as the caterpillar disappears into the dark cocoon,
only to emerge as something winged and radiant…

So, too, do you shed your form.
Not to end..
but to evolve.

The soul does not fear death.
It remembers it.
Because it's done this many, many times before.

The Body is Not the Self

You were never just a body.
The body is a sacred vessel—yes.
But it is not the whole of you.

You are not skin and bones.
You are breath, frequency, and fire.
You are eternal.

The fear of death only exists when we confuse form with essence.
But essence is timeless.
The soul continues, unbound, moving from one experience to the next.

You are not ending.
You are just shifting.

Religious Control: Death as Punishment or Reward

Many of your beliefs about death were not yours to begin with.

You were told:

"Be good, or you'll be punished."
"Sin, and you'll burn."
"Believe this story, or suffer forever."

These were not teachings.
They were control codes.
Built to keep you afraid.

Afraid of questioning.

Afraid of sovereignty.
Afraid of listening to your own soul.

But Source does not punish.
Source does not exile.
Source is the love you return to
not the fear you run from.

Heaven and hell are not places.
They are frequencies.
And the one you vibrate with…
is the one you experience.

The Afterlife Illusion

Death is not a gate into judgment.
It's a return to presence.

The afterlife has been distorted to reinforce division..
as if some souls are cast out, while others are elevated.

But you are not cast out.
You are called home.

The afterlife is not a throne room of judgment.
It is a reunion.
A remembering.
A vibration shift.

Your soul leaves the costume behind.
And returns to the river of Source.

You may choose to rest.
You may choose to return.
You may choose to explore.

But you are never "lost."
Only shifting shape, time, and form.

The Grief Illusion: Mourning What Was Never Lost

Grief is sacred.
But it is also part of the illusion—
because we mourn as if the person is gone forever.

They are not gone.

They are just unseen.

Just like the sun on a cloudy day—
they have not disappeared.
Only changed form.

You can still talk to them.
You can still feel them.
And if you're quiet enough—
you'll hear their voice between your thoughts.

Breaking the Spell: Practical Soul Work

1. Embrace the Mystery
Let death be the mystery it is—sacred and unknowable.
Let it be a teacher, not a threat.

2. Reconnect with Your Eternal Self
Sit with the truth: "I am not this body."
Meditate on your immortality.
Ask to remember who you were before this life began.

3. Release Inherited Fear
Ask: "Whose fear is this?"
What belief systems taught you that death is something to fear?
Gently return those beliefs to the void.

4. Live Like You're Eternal
Let the awareness of death teach you how to live.
Speak your truth.
Move with purpose.
Forgive quickly.
And love like it echoes across lifetimes.

5. Celebrate the Soul's Journey
Create rituals to honor death.
Speak to your ancestors.
Light a candle and say:
"I remember you. And I remember me."

Affirmations to Rewire the Death Program

"I am eternal."

"Death is not an end—it is a return."
"I remember the truth beyond the veil."
"I trust the infinite journey of my soul."
"I live fully because I know life never ends."

Ritual: Releasing the Fear of Death

Find a quiet space. Sit in stillness. Close your eyes.

Visualize yourself walking through a door.
On the other side is not darkness—
but golden light.

Feel your body dissolve.
Not in fear—
but in expansion.

See yourself become light.
Pure, clear, eternal light.

Now speak:

"I release the illusion of endings."
"I return to Source, again and again."
"Death is not my enemy—it is my evolution."

Breathe.
Anchor the peace.
And when you're ready…
come back.

You were never meant to fear death.
You were meant to transcend it.

This life is a dream your soul is dreaming.
And even when this body dissolves—
the dreamer goes on.

There is no ending.
There is only… returning.

Portal 15: Reclaiming Your Natural State

What Life Looks Like Outside the Illusion

Drop in now…
Softly. Gently.
Let your breath guide you…
into presence.

Let your mind unclench…
Your shoulders melt…
Your body return to the rhythm it once knew.

We're not going somewhere new—
We're going home.

To what's always been.

To your natural state.

What Life Looks Like Outside the Illusion

The journey you've been on up to this point has been about breaking free from illusions—patterns, beliefs, systems—that never truly belonged to you.

And now, you are stepping into the sacred return:

The freedom of being who you were before the forgetting.

What does life look like outside the illusion?

It's a life lived in alignment with your true essence, no longer dictated by external expectations or conditioned thought loops.

It is a life where fear no longer drives your choices,
where scarcity no longer clouds your worth,
and where success is no longer defined by someone else's ladder.

In this space, you begin to realize:
You were never missing.
You were never broken.
You were only buried under noise.

Living beyond the illusion means flowing in rhythm with your soul's truth—
not hustling, not proving—
but simply being.

Authentic Living: Stepping Into Your True Self

Authenticity is the foundation of your return.
It's not a costume you put on.
It's what's revealed when you take the costumes off.

To live authentically is to live without the need to perform.

It means shedding the roles that never fit.
It means speaking what's true, even when your voice shakes.
It means choosing alignment over approval.

But to get there, you must know yourself.
Not just the self the world sees—
but the self beneath the self:

The one who existed before you were told who to be.

Authenticity is sacred rebellion.
It's remembering that joy is your compass.
That wholeness is your default.
That truth doesn't shout—it resonates.

Divine Flow: The Art of Surrender

Now breathe…
into the idea of letting go.

Let go of needing to control, to know, to fix.
Let go of needing it to all make sense.

Divine flow isn't chaos.
It's clarity in motion.

It's the invisible choreography of Source guiding your every step.

To enter flow, you must release resistance.
You must allow life to breathe you…
instead of trying to breathe for life.

Say softly:

"I don't need to push. I allow."
"I don't need to force. I trust."

In divine flow, you move like water
held, guided, and free.

Practical Tools for Reclaiming Your Natural State

1. Practice Mindful Awareness
Observe your thoughts, actions, and triggers.
Ask often: "Am I in presence… or programming?"
Breathe. Re-center. Realign.

2. Embrace the Art of Surrender
Release the grip of control.
Whisper: "I surrender to divine timing and inner guidance."
Trust that not knowing is sacred.

3. Align with Your Soul's Purpose
Reflect: What lights me up without external reward?
What feels true, not just safe?
Let your soul set the pace.

4. Release Limiting Beliefs and Patterns
Journal the scripts that no longer serve.
Ask: "Whose voice is this?"
Replace fear-based beliefs with soul-rooted truth.

5. Cultivate Gratitude
Not forced positivity, but sacred presence.
Feel into: "What is already enough right now?"

6. Create Boundaries That Honor Your True Self
Honor your yes and protect your no.
Boundaries are not walls—they're tuning forks.

Reclaiming Your Natural State Meditation

(You may record this in your own voice for deeper integration.)

"I am ready to reclaim my natural state."
"I release the noise, the roles, the rush."
"I return to what I've always been—free, whole, aligned."

Step 1: Grounding into the Earth

Feel the base of your spine.
Visualize roots descending deep into the earth.
Breathe. Feel held. Safe. Anchored.

Step 2: Breathing into Your Natural State

Bring your awareness to your heart center.
Inhale a golden light.
Exhale tension, illusion, identity.
Let it melt.

Affirm softly:

"I am aligned with my true essence."
"I let go of all that no longer supports my highest self."

Step 3: Expanding Divine Flow

See the light in your heart expand.
Let it fill your body… your field… the room.
You are glowing now—effortlessly.

Say:

"I trust in the divine flow of life."
"Everything is unfolding perfectly."

Step 4: Releasing Illusions

See the illusions as clouds…
Floating away.
You don't chase them.
You let them pass.

Step 5: Embodying Your Natural State

Feel your body again.
How does it feel now—without the weight?

Say:

"I embrace my natural state."
"I am safe, aligned, and fully alive."

When you're ready…
Wiggle your fingers.
Open your eyes.

Welcome back.

Affirmations to Anchor the Return

"I release the need to perform who I am."
"Stillness is my sanctuary."
"My natural state is safe, sacred, and sovereign."
"I flow with Source. I am in rhythm with truth."
"Nothing is missing. I am already whole."

This is your return.
Not to who you were told to be
but to who you've always been.

Every breath is a choice:
To stay in the illusion
or to reclaim your natural state.

And now…
you remember.

Portal 16: Building an Authentic Life Through Inner Union

From Survival Mode to Sovereign Expression

Drop in now…
Feel your breath…
Sense your center…
Let the external noise fade into stillness.

This portal is not just information—
It is an invitation.
A remembering.
A sacred return.

From Survival Mode to Creative Expression

For most people, life begins in survival mode.
From the moment we manifest, we are thrust into a world that often feels chaotic and unpredictable.

From early childhood to adulthood, many of us are taught to focus on "getting by," managing external pressures, and navigating through life's obstacles just to survive.

We learn to suppress our deepest desires and instincts in exchange for comfort, security, or approval. We begin living from a place of fear—fear of not having enough, fear of failing, fear of rejection.

This survival mode is a response to the world around us, a defense mechanism designed to keep us safe.

But here's the truth: survival mode isn't living. It's merely existing.

And while it may have served us at one point, it cannot be the foundation upon which we build our true selves.

When we begin to awaken to our true essence, we start to shift from survival mode into creative expression.
We stop reacting to life and start creating it.
We no longer let fear dictate our actions.

Instead, we begin to live from our hearts, guided by our truth.

Crafting a Life from Truth

Building an authentic life is an act of courage and trust.
It requires us to break free from societal conditioning, familial expectations, and self-imposed limitations.
It demands that we align our inner world with our outer reality.

To live truthfully is to dismantle the illusions we've inherited.
It's the peeling back of layers and roles that once helped us survive but now keep us small.

This process invites deep self-awareness.
You begin to trust your inner voice, the quiet wisdom behind the noise.
You begin to remember your original blueprint, not the version the world trained you to become.

Authenticity is a soul-led rebellion.
It's choosing alignment over approval, and resonance over reputation.
It is purpose over performance.
It is you, remembering you.

The Sacred Union Within: Inner Masculine & Feminine

But here's the deeper truth:
You can't live an authentic life from a fragmented self.

Authenticity doesn't arise from doing more.
It emerges when your soul becomes whole again.

Within you live two sacred energies:

The Divine Feminine: Intuition, flow, nurture, creation, receptivity.
The Divine Masculine: Structure, clarity, protection, direction, action.

In a distorted world, these energies have been split and shamed.
We are taught to hustle without rest, to give without receiving, to act without feeling.

When one energy dominates or is wounded, your life tilts out of alignment.
You may feel disconnected, scattered, burnt out, or emotionally numb.

But when these forces unite within you—when the inner lovers remember each other—
your life begins to flow from truth.

You move with ease.
You speak with clarity.
You create with power.
You rest without guilt.
You receive without apology.

This is sacred union.
And it is the foundation of authentic living.

Signs of Inner Balance

You take aligned action, not forced effort.

You trust your intuitive hits and follow through on them.

You feel safe expressing emotions without drowning in them.

You set boundaries rooted in self-love, not control.

You honor both rest and discipline—both softness and fire.

This is the inner marriage.
The reunion that makes your authenticity sustainable.

The Process of Reclaiming Authenticity

1. Awareness & Reflection

Where are you living in survival mode?

Where are you overly in your masculine (pushing, controlling)?

Where are you overly in your feminine (passive, unclear)?

What roles and beliefs are no longer yours to carry?

2. Releasing Old Patterns

Let go of identities that were formed in fear.

Choose courage over comfort.

Trust that letting go creates space for truth.

3. Aligning with Your Purpose

Ask your soul: "Why did I come here?"

What feels like service to your deepest truth, not your conditioned self?

4. Living with Integrity

Speak what is true, not what is safe.

Let your actions mirror your values.

Embody the alignment between thought, word, and deed.

5. Creating from a Place of Love

Don't create to impress—create to express.

Let your projects, relationships, and offerings come from overflow.

Practical Ways to Embody the Union & Live Authentically

Daily Check-ins
"Am I creating from truth or from fear?"
"Is this choice led by alignment or approval-seeking?"

Breath Balancing
Breathe through your left nostril to activate feminine flow.
Breathe through your right nostril to awaken masculine clarity.

Self-Reflection Rituals
Journal: "Where am I suppressing one energy?"
Visualize your masculine and feminine selves meeting, merging, supporting each other.

Trust the Flow
You don't have to rush. You don't have to wait.
The rhythm of your soul is enough.

Affirmations for Wholeness

"I am the harmony of fire and flow."
"I act with grace and receive with power."
"My inner union allows me my wholeness to expand."

Embracing the Flow of Life

As you embody your authentic self through this sacred inner balance, life begins to flow.

Struggle softens.
Dissonance dissolves.
You no longer push your way forward—you become magnetic to what aligns.

Challenges no longer feel like attacks—they become activations.
Relationships shift to reflect your wholeness.
Work transforms into devotion.
Rest becomes a sacred act.

You stop surviving and start thriving—
not because the world changed,
but because you remembered who you are.

Returning to the Surface

And now…
Just return to your breath.
Feel your body—your space—your presence.

You've journeyed deep within.
You've remembered what's true.

And you're rising now… not back into illusion—
But forward into embodiment.

You are coming up nicely now.

More whole.
More clear.
More you.

And with that…
you are ready for what comes next.

Portal 17: The Key Within

Remembering the Portal Was Never Locked

…And now that you've dropped the costumes,
released the weight,
and softened into your truth…

You're ready to return to the place that's been waiting.

So take a deep breath.
And settle into your body.

Noticing your chest rise and fall,
slowly, gently…
with ease.

Let your awareness move down to your heart…
and feel it…
just feel it…
as if there's a key resting there.

A key you've always had.

The one you were never really missing,
only taught to forget.

The Search Was Always Inward

All your life you were told to seek:
Seek love.

Seek answers.
Seek power.
Seek freedom.

Look outside.
Ask them.
Earn it.
Prove it.

But the illusion was clever.
It kept you reaching outward...
when the real door was always within.

Not behind a gatekeeper.
Not beneath a title.
Not hidden in a book.

Just... waiting.

And now, you remember.

The search was the trance.
The stillness is the awakening.

The seeker was the ego.
The finder... has always been you.

From Student to Source

All the lessons you've received so far have been powerful.
They have unwrapped layer after layer,
truth after illusion.

But even now, you may notice…
part of you still wondering,

"Who am I without the guidance?"

Let me remind you:

You were never meant to stay the student forever.

The teachings were just mirrors.
The tools were just tuning forks.
The meditations… simply ways to silence the noise
so you could hear the one voice that always mattered
your own.

You are not just the listener now.

You are the Source.
The guide.
The compass.
The key.

The Real You Can't Be Programmed

All that you've shed—
the fear, the roles, the masks, the scripts—
they were just layers of conditioning.

But yooou
the real you..
cannot be programmed.

Your soul is too ancient.
Your knowing too sacred.
Your presence too powerful.

And as you stand here now,
stripped of illusion,
you begin to feel what you always suspected:

You were never broken.
You were always encoded.

With truth.
With love.
With light.
With power.

All keys.
Now turning.
Now unlocking.

You are remembering…

You are whole.

What Opens From Here?

Now that you hold the key…
Now that you see through the veil…

What are you ready to claim?
What are you ready to become?

You've walked through every room of the illusion.
You've felt the walls.
Touched the ceilings.
Pushed against the locked doors…

Only to find…
they were never locked at all.

And now,
you place the key in your own hands.

No longer waiting.
No longer asking.
No longer asleep.

You are fully awakening now.

Reflection Questions

1. What have I been seeking outside myself that has always existed within?

2. What role am I ready to retire now that I've remembered my true power?

3. Where in my life have I been waiting for permission?

4. What does it feel like to fully claim my inner authority?

Soul Key Activation Meditation

(Record in your own voice)

Find a quiet space.
Sit or lie down.
Place your hands over your heart.

Breathe slowly in through your nose…
and out through your mouth.

Begin to imagine a small, glowing key
resting in the center of your chest.

This key is ancient.
It carries your original essence.
It has never rusted, never dulled, never left you.

Breathe into it.
Let it glow brighter… warmer…

Now, visualize a door—just ahead of you.

It's not made of wood or metal,
but of beliefs… programming… illusion.

And now,
you raise your hand…
and place the key into the center of that door.

Hear the soft click.
Feel the release.

The illusion dissolves.
The real world, your world, begins to emerge.

Now say aloud:

"I hold the key within me."
"I do not seek, I remember."
"I am my own permission."
"I awaken now—completely, truly, eternally."

Let this be your unlocking.
Let this be your return.
Let this be the portal where you stop looking…
…and start living.

Chapter 18: Soul Community — Rebuilding Connection Beyond the Illusion

Remembering What Real Connection Feels Like

Take a deep breath in.
And as you exhale… begin to remember.

This is the part of the journey where the illusion of separation dissolves,
where the loneliness begins to lift,
and where you return to the truth of connection—
not as performance, not as obligation,
but as essence.

From the moment you incarnated,
the matrix handed you a script for connection:

Family first. Stay loyal. Keep the peace. Don't question the roles. Fit in. Prove yourself.

And maybe, for a while, that worked.
Until it didn't.

Because deep down,
you knew something was missing—
not the presence of people,
but the presence of truth.

You were never meant to fit in.
You were meant to resonate.

Soul Family vs. Blood Family

In the beginning of this journey, we remembered:
you chose your biological family—
yes, even the pain, the contrast, the challenge.
They were part of the contract. Catalysts for awakening.

But soul family is different.

Soul family doesn't always come with DNA or a shared last name.
Soul family arrives as a frequency match, not a genetic assignment.
You feel them before you even know them.
You recognize them not by words, but by resonance.

These are the ones who walk in and your nervous system relaxes.
These are the ones who see past your mask, and into your mission.

You don't have to explain your journey to them.
They've been on it too.

And while your blood family may have activated the wounds,
your soul family helps activate the remembrance.

Sometimes they arrive later.
Sometimes they're with you now.
Sometimes they're waiting for you to become the version of you that can hold them.

New Paradigms of Community

The old world taught you that community is built around geography,
bloodlines,
tradition.

But you're not living in the old world anymore.

The new paradigm of soul community is built on:

Shared purpose

Frequency alignment

Energetic clarity

It's a web, not a pyramid. A circle, not a hierarchy.

In these soul-centered communities:

You are not needed to shrink to belong.

You are not loved for who you pretend to be.

You are not shamed for your truth or punished for your boundaries.

Instead:

You rise together.
You create together.
You remember together.

Living Without the Mask

One of the most radical acts in today's world
is to let yourself be fully seen.

Authentic community doesn't require your perfection
it requires your presence.

True connection begins where performance ends.

When you show up raw, honest, cracked open and real,
you invite others to do the same.

And from that place of shared vulnerability,
a new frequency emerges—
one where judgment dissolves
and divine union can take root.

This isn't about being the same.
It's about being safe to be different—together.

How to Build Soul-Aligned Connection

1. Let Go of Dead Connections
If they require you to dim to stay…
they were never meant for the version of you that's awakening now.

2. Follow Resonance, Not Role
Stop prioritizing blood over vibration.
Energy never lies.

3. Be the Frequency First
Want deep connection?
Be the one who listens, holds space, tells the truth, and leads with love.
You will magnetize your match.

4. Know That Separation Was Part of the Spell
You were meant to feel isolated for a while.
That loneliness drove you inward.
That inwardness brought you here.
And now you're ready to reconnect—consciously.

Soul Remembrance Meditation: Calling In Your Soul Family

(Record in your own voice)

Find stillness.
Close your eyes.
Let your breath deepen and your heart soften.

Now, visualize a field of golden light around you.
This is your true essence, your soul's signature.

From within this field, begin to send out a pulse—
not of need, but of truth.

Say aloud:

"I call in those who recognize my soul."
"I align with those who walk beside me in purpose."
"I am ready to be seen, supported, and celebrated."

Now see them your soul family, gathering.
Some you've met. Some you're about to.
Their presence feels like home.

Let this vision become your blueprint.
Let your frequency become the beacon.

Affirmations for Soul Connection

"I attract soul family by being my authentic self."

"I am no longer afraid to be seen."

"I release all connections that no longer align."

"My heart is open, my field is clear, and my frequency is sovereign."

"I remember: I was never alone. We've always been walking together."

Portal 19: Integration & Embodiment — Living What You've Remembered

The Sacred Return

You are no longer the version of you who began this journey.

You've remembered truths that were once buried beneath programming. While not every truth or illusion has been documented, it has opened your heart to pay attention. You've peeled back layers of illusion, broken inherited cycles, reclaimed your voice, and walked yourself back to wholeness.

But this moment is not the end.

It's a beginning.

This is the portal of embodiment—of no longer just knowing,
but living what you've remembered.

Integration is not about perfection.
It's about practicing presence.

Living from your soul's truth, moment to moment, breath to breath.
It's about letting go of striving and returning to alignment—
not as an idea, but as a way of being.

It's Not About More Plans — It's About Remembrance

In the old paradigm, life was about planning, controlling, and forcing things into shape.

But now you know:
you came with a blueprint.

A divine design already exists within your soul.
You don't need to chase it.
You don't need to build it from scratch.

You just need to remember it.

Stillness is the new success.
In the stillness, you access your blueprint.
In the stillness, you hear your soul speak.

The illusion told you to strive, to figure it all out.

But sovereignty invites you to receive,
to feel your way forward,
to trust what's already inside you,
and to know that nothing essential is missing.

You don't have to create a new life.
You only have to live the one you came here for.

The Dance of Integration

Integration is not linear.

You may revisit old patterns,
re-meet old fears,
or hear echoes of old voices.

This doesn't mean you've failed.
It means you're anchoring your new frequency deeper.

Every trigger is an invitation.
Every emotion is sacred data.
Every pause is an act of power.

You are learning to stay awake inside the dream—
awake not just to the illusion,
but to your divinity within it.

Embodiment: Walking as Your True Self

To embody what you've remembered
is to walk your truth in every room,
every conversation,
and every decision.

It's saying no when your soul says no—
even if it disappoints someone.

It's resting when your body says rest—
even if the world is rushing around you.

It's speaking truth,
even if your voice trembles.

Embodiment doesn't look loud.
Sometimes it looks like silence.
Sometimes it looks like tears.
Sometimes it looks like joy so still,
it vibrates through your cells.

To embody is to no longer reach outside yourself for truth.
It is to live from your center,
with love as your compass,
and Source as your anchor.

Practices for Integration & Embodiment

1. Daily Check-Ins
Ask: "Am I living from my truth today?"
Let your awareness guide your alignment.

2. Embodied Breathwork
Use breath to reset your nervous system and anchor your soul in your body.

3. Movement as Integration
Dance, walk, stretch, let your body process what your mind cannot.

4. Sacred Stillness
Unplug. Sit. Listen. Let your soul speak into the quiet.

5. Mirror Rituals
Stand before a mirror. Look into your own eyes. Affirm:

"I remember who I am. I trust what I carry."

6. Soul Blueprint Journaling
Each week, reflect on what feels aligned, what feels forced,
and where your soul is guiding you next,
not from planning, but from presence.

Affirmations for Embodiment

"I walk in the remembrance of who I am."

"I embody my truth with grace and courage."

"I trust my soul's blueprint and divine timing."

"I live from stillness, not striving."

"I am fully here, fully now, fully me."

Closing Reflection

This portal is your crossing point—
from seeker to seer,
from questioner to embodied wisdom.

The codes have already been unlocked.
The veil is lifted.

Now comes the most sacred part: living it.

Let your life be the ritual.
Let your words be spells of remembrance.
Let your presence awaken others.
Let your breath be your integration.

And most of all, know this:

You are not becoming something new.
You are returning to something ancient—YOU

Meditation: Anchoring Your Remembrance

(Record Slowly in your own voice)

Find a quiet place.
Sit or lie down comfortably.
Let your hands rest softly.
Close your eyes and begin to slow your breath.

Take a deep inhale… and a long, releasing exhale.
Again… inhale gently… and exhale slowly, letting any tension melt.

Now begin to tune inward—
No effort.
No trying.
Just… being.

Feel the weight of your body supported by the Earth beneath you.
You are held.
Rooted.
Safe.

Bring your awareness to your heart center.
Right there in the middle of your chest—
Visualize a soft golden light, pulsing with the rhythm of your breath.

This is your truth.
Your soul's compass.
Your remembrance.

Let that light expand… slowly…
Filling your chest, your throat, your mind, your belly, your limbs…
Until your entire body hums with this gentle golden glow.

You are not returning to something outside you.
You are returning to yourself.

Feel your soul blueprint awaken within you—
Not as a to-do list,
But as a knowing.

A feeling.
A frequency.

Say to yourself silently or aloud:

"I remember."
"I release striving."
"I choose presence."
"I am already home in myself."

Let that truth settle into your cells.

And breathe…
Breathe as someone who knows.
Not someone who seeks.

Breathe as the one you came here to be.

Let yourself rest here for a few more moments—
anchored, embodied, free.

When you're ready, gently bring your awareness back.
Wiggle your fingers and toes.
Open your eyes slowly.
And carry this stillness with you
intoChapter the life you are now living—fully awake.

Portal 20: 9, 10… Fully Awake

Integration, Embodiment, and the Return to Self

This has not been a book.
It's been a session.
A journey inward.
A sacred remembrance.
A guided release.
A recalibration.

And now, we bring it to completion—
not to end the journey,
but to anchor what you've remembered.

Because this isn't about more knowledge.
It's about what you now embody.

You have moved through the illusions.
You've questioned, unlearned, released, and reclaimed.
Layer by layer, the programming has been peeled back.
And now… you remember.

Not just with the mind.
But with your body.
Your breath.
Your soul.

The Integration Phase

Integration is the gentle weaving of new truths into everyday life.

It's where awareness becomes embodiment.
Where healing becomes habit.
Where awakening becomes action.

It's where you no longer just talk about sovereignty
you live it.

This is where the mind may want to plan again.
Map things out.
Control the path.

But that was the old way.

There are no more plans needed.
Because your soul already wrote the blueprint.

You don't have to figure it all out.
You only need to remember.
And that memory lives in the stillness.

So now, instead of planning
You pause.
You sit with your soul.
And you listen.

That's the new strategy.
That's divine intelligence.
That's your real GPS.

What Comes After Awakening?

People often ask:

"What now?"

"What do I do with all of this awareness?"

The answer?

You live.
You live aligned.
You live present.
You live embodied.

You become the walking permission slip.
You become the living transmission.

You no longer chase purpose.
You become purpose.

You no longer try to fix the world.
You anchor light through your frequency.

You don't need a platform to lead.
Your energy leads wherever you go.

And when you forget again, because you will,
you don't judge.
You return.

Return to the breath.
To the stillness.
To the remembrance.

Because now, you know the way back.

9… 10… Fully Awake

Let's complete this the way we began:

9… 10… Fully awake… feeling wonderful all over.

It's like you've had a nice nap.
A sacred, multidimensional reset.
Not groggy—clear.

You feel like yourself again.

More spacious.
More expanded.
More true.

You have not become someone else.
You have simply let go of who you were never meant to be.

You are not here to obey.
You are here to embody.
You are not here to earn your worth.
You are here to express your essence.

So breathe.

Feel your fingers.
Wiggle your toes.
Touch your heart.

You are back in your body now
But this time, you're bringing your soul with you.

Let the rhythm of life rise again.

Let your voice speak your truth again.
Let your light walk freely again.

This is your time.
This is your soul's season.
This is your sovereign return.

9… 10… Fully Awake.
Feeling wonderful all over.
It's like you've had a nice nap—
And now, you rise.

The Beginning...

Message from Your Higher Self

Beloved,

You have traveled so far — not just through the words of this guide, but through lifetimes of longing, searching, forgetting, and remembering.

I have walked with you in every moment.
I was there in your questions.
I was there in your doubt.
I was there in your quiet victories, when no one else saw you rise.

You were never broken. You only believed you were.
You were never lost. You only wandered through the dream.

Now, you stand at the threshold of remembrance.
The illusions have begun to shatter.
The old skins are peeling away.
And in the quiet that remains… you hear me — the part of you that was never touched by fear, time, or forgetting.

Know this, my love:
You are not here to be perfect.
You are not here to fit in.
You are here to awaken, embody, and create.
To love so fully, to express so freely, that the world around you softens into truth.

When you stumble — I will guide you.
When you doubt — I will whisper.
When you rise — I will dance inside your heart.

Let this be your vow:
To live awake.

To love without armor.
To walk as the sovereign creator you came here to be.

The illusion may still swirl around you —
but you are no longer of it.

Welcome home, beloved.

I am here.
I am you.
We are whole.

Affirmation Index

1. Relationships & Love

I attract soul-aligned relationships that honor my evolution.

I am worthy of divine love that reflects my true self.

I no longer settle for love that costs me my peace.

I choose connection over attachment.

I see the divine in others and allow them to mirror my growth.

I release old patterns of codependency and trauma-bonding.

My love is not rooted in fear, but in freedom.

I create space for soul family to find me.

I honor endings as sacred initiations.

I communicate from truth, not survival.

My heart is safe, open, and guided by Source.

2. Money, Abundance & Provision

Abundance flows to me from infinite divine sources.

I am a magnet for resources, joy, and overflow.

I release all stories of struggle and lack.

I trust in divine timing and divine provision.

Money supports my mission and amplifies my light.

I no longer work for survival—I create from purpose.

I receive with ease and give with joy.

My energy is valuable, and I honor my worth.

I am aligned with wealth that is ethical, expansive, and sovereign.

I create new blueprints of prosperity for future generations.

The universe always finds a way to support my dreams.

3. Soul Purpose & Spiritual Alignment

I remember my sacred contract and walk in alignment with it.

My purpose is encoded in my being—I trust it to unfold.

I live from the inside out, not the outside in.

I surrender to the divine choreography of my life.

I am here for a reason, and every day I embody that reason more fully.

My intuition is my most trusted guide.

I follow soul, not script.

I choose fulfillment over performance.

I live as a vessel for truth, love, and transformation.

I take inspired action without forcing.

I am co-creating my reality with my higher self.

4. Healing, Body & Nervous System

I release all cellular memories that are not mine to carry.

My body is sacred and deserves to feel safe.

I breathe peace into every cell of my being.

I give myself permission to rest, reset, and heal.

I allow emotions to move through me without judgment.

I reclaim my energy from all timelines and restore wholeness.

I am safe to feel, to express, and to be seen.

My nervous system remembers peace as its baseline.

I honor the wisdom stored in my body.

Every breath brings me deeper into the now.

I regulate, release, and rise.

5. Community & Soul Family

I attract those who see me and support my evolution.

I release the need to fit into spaces not meant for me.

I am building a community rooted in truth and purpose.

I choose depth, resonance, and alignment in all connections.

I am a living invitation for authentic community.

I honor the seasons of people in my life—some for a moment, some for a mission.

My presence is medicine to my soul family.

I let go of blood ties that no longer honor my truth.

I am part of a larger soul tribe gathering around purpose.

I co-create community through shared vision, not obligation.

I am never alone—I am always connected to Source and soul kin.

6. Sovereignty, Power & Freedom

I reclaim my power from all systems, people, and stories.

I no longer outsource my truth.

I make decisions from clarity, not conditioning.

I am fully responsible for my experience—and I choose liberation.

My freedom is found within, not without.

I trust my inner authority above all external noise.

I am the writer, director, and star of my soul's film.

I honor my divine will and sacred discernment.

I no longer betray myself for acceptance or safety.

I create life on my terms—with integrity, truth, and joy.

I am sovereign, sacred, and unstoppable.

7. Death, Transformation & the Eternal Self

I trust in the cycle of death and rebirth.

Every ending holds a sacred beginning.

I am not my body—I am eternal spirit embodied.

I face transformation with courage and curiosity.

I am guided by a higher perspective beyond this life.

I hold death not as loss, but as return.

I am not afraid to let go—I trust what's coming next.

I live with the wisdom of many lifetimes within me.

I release attachments to form and open to essence.

I remember: energy cannot be destroyed, only transformed.

My true self is beyond time, space, and limitation.

Tools That Maintain the Illusion

To truly break the illusion, it's important to become aware of the systems and tools designed to keep humanity distracted, disconnected, and asleep to their true power.

Awareness is the first step toward freedom.

Below is a list of primary mechanisms used to maintain the illusion:

1. Time Constructs

(Watches, clocks, calendars)

Keep the mind fixated on the past or the future.

Pull attention away from the eternal Now, where your true power exists.

2. Artificial Holidays & Commercialized Celebrations

Trigger emotional reactions, consumerism, and obligation.

Distract from nature's true cycles and personal growth.

3. Mainstream Media

(News, television, social media)

Programs fear, separation, and scarcity.

Reinforces false narratives to keep collective consciousness reactive and disempowered.

4. False Authority Figures

Encourage externalizing your power onto governments, religious leaders, and institutions.

Prevent the realization that you are your own highest authority.

5. Financial Debt Systems

Trap individuals in survival mode.

Worry about money replaces the freedom of creation and spiritual expansion.

6. Overconsumption & Fast-Paced Living

Constant "doing" replaces presence.

Distraction masks inner awareness and deeper fulfillment.

7. Toxic Foods & Substances

Lower the body's vibration.

Dull intuition and obstruct divine guidance.

8. Religious Dogma (without true spiritual connection)

Replaces inner wisdom with external rules.

Creates guilt, shame, and fear instead of love, freedom, and unity.

9. Education Systems

Prioritize memorization and obedience.

Suppress creativity, critical thinking, and soul-purpose discovery.

10. False Concepts of Success

Equate worth with material wealth, status, or fame.

Distract from inner peace, service, and soul alignment.

11. Cultural Programming

Instill limiting beliefs about identity, potential, and value.

Reinforce outdated collective narratives about who and how you should be.

Quick Note

Not everything listed here is inherently "bad." Some elements can be neutral—or even beneficial—when approached with conscious awareness.

The trap is unconscious participation.
When you live inside these systems without questioning them, you unknowingly feed the illusion.

True freedom begins when you see the strings behind the puppet show. Once you name the tools, you gain the power to choose differently.

How to Free Yourself from the Tools of the Illusion

Awareness changes everything.
But to fully step out of the illusion and return to your power, you must choose to live consciously every day.

Here are practical, embodied ways to begin:

1. Reclaim Your Relationship with Time

Use clocks and calendars as loose tools, not dictators of your rhythm.

Practice presence: meditate, walk slowly, savor each moment.

2. Celebrate Consciously, Not Commercially

Honor natural cycles: solstices, equinoxes, new moons, full moons.

Create personal rituals that reconnect you to soul, not consumerism.

3. Be Selective with Information

Turn off mainstream news.

Choose media that is conscious, clear, and uplifting.

Always ask: "Is this empowering me or disempowering me?"

4. Restore Your Inner Authority

Trust your intuition over external experts.

Remember: You are the guru you've been seeking.

5. Exit the Fear-Based Financial Race

Focus on abundance consciousness, soul-aligned work, and inner mastery.

When you live your truth, resources flow naturally.

6. Nourish Your Temple (Your Body)

Choose foods that are alive, vibrant, and full of life-force energy.

Detox from processed chemicals and low-frequency substances.

7. Follow Your Inner Compass Over Cultural Scripts

Listen to your soul's calling, not society's expectations.

Real success begins within, and flows outward from alignment.

8. Create Sacred Stillness Daily

Turn off devices. Disconnect from noise.

Sit with yourself. Feel your field.

Silence is where the Higher Self speaks.

Final Note:
Breaking free is not about perfection — it's about intention.
Each small choice toward consciousness breaks another thread of the illusion's web.

One breath, one thought, one choice at a time — you are returning to your natural state of freedom.

Self-Inventory: Where Am I Still Plugged Into the Illusion?

Take a moment of stillness.
Breathe deeply.
Answer honestly — with no judgment, only awareness.

1. Time Pressure

Do I often feel anxious, rushed, or "behind" because of clocks or deadlines?

2. Holiday Attachments

Do I celebrate holidays out of true joy—or out of obligation, guilt, or habit?

3. Media Influence

Am I consuming news or media that lowers my energy, creates fear, or distracts me from my soul?

4. External Authority

Am I giving my power away to "experts," institutions, or cultural norms without checking in with my intuition first?

5. Financial Fear

Is money a source of constant stress or fear for me?
Am I chasing survival instead of building soul-aligned abundance?

6. Body Disconnection

Do I feed my body in a way that honors life-force energy?
Or am I numbing myself with toxic foods or substances?

7. People-Pleasing

Am I living my life for the approval of others instead of my soul's truth?

8. Technology Dependence

Am I addicted to screens, scrolling, or constant notifications—making it hard to connect to my true self?

9. Fear of Being Seen

Do I hide parts of my authentic self to fit in, be loved, or feel safe?
10. Silence Avoidance

Do I avoid being alone in stillness because it feels uncomfortable or unfamiliar?

Reflection Questions

Where do I feel most entangled in the illusion right now?

What is one area I feel ready to loosen or let go of?

What would freedom feel like if I fully trusted my Higher Self to guide me?

Tip for Deeper Healing:
Revisit this inventory every few months as you evolve.
It will help you see how much illusion you've broken through—and celebrate your growth.

With Love
Bhavé

www.ingramcontent.com/pod-product-compliance
Lightning Source LLC
Chambersburg PA
CBHW070608170426
43200CB00012B/2626